A GUIDE TO
GREETING CARD WRITING

edited by
Larry Sandman

Writer's Digest Books

Cincinnati, Ohio

This book is an extensive revision, rewrite, and update of a book originally titled *The Greeting Card Writer's Handbook.*

Second printing 1984
Third printing 1985

Library of Congress Cataloging in Publication Data

Writer's Digest Books (Firm)
    A guide to greeting card writing.
    Edition of 1968 published under title: The greeting card writer's handbook.
    Bibliography: p.
    Includes index.
    1. Greeting cards—Authorship. I. Sandman, Larry. II. Greeting card writer's handbook. III. Title.
N171.G74G8 1980   808.1'8   80-19737
    ISBN 0-89879-141-3

Design by Barron Krody

Acknowledgments

Grateful acknowledgment is made to the following companies for permission to reprint greeting card verses:

American Greetings, Charmcraft Publishers, Freedom Greetings, The Paramount Line, Inc., Rust Craft Cards, Sunshine Art Studios, and Warner Press Publishers—for verses by Patricia Ann Emme appearing in Chapter 5, "Writing the Inspirational Verse."

Gibson Greeting Cards, Inc., for verses appearing throughout the book.

Norcross, for verses appearing in Chapter 7, "Light and Bright . . . Informals."

The Paramount Line, Inc., for verses by Bernice Gourse appearing in Chapter 4, "Personal Relationship Cards."

Rust Craft Greeting Cards, Inc., for verses from its Rust Craft and Barker lines appearing throughout the book.

Editor's Note

In the four years since the first edition of *A Guide to Greeting Card Writing* was published, the card industry has undergone a lot of changes. The number of major companies buying freelance ideas has declined. At the same time, the number of freelance writers attempting to sell greeting cards has increased, making it more and more difficult for new writers to break into the market.

In order to succeed today, you must really stand out. You need talent, professionalism, and perseverance, but more than all that, you need knowledge. You have to know how to write, what to write, and where to sell it. This book can help you increase your knowledge of how and what to write. Reading it will not make you an instant star, but it will give you the edge over those who plunge into the market blindly.

For information on where to sell, see the list of greeting card companies in the current *Writer's Market*.

Now more than ever harried editors are in need of writers who can produce consistently outstanding cards. If you are one of those special people, then this book is for you. I hope you find it a helpful tool that will enable you to compete successfully in this challenging market.

Larry Sandman

Contents

mood. Getting the customer to identify. Examples of personal relationship cards.

5. Writing the Inspirational Verse 61
by Patricia Ann Emme

Origins of inspirational greeting cards. Two well-known writers. Inspirational vs. conventional verse. Examples of good inspirationals. Importance of sendability. Sources of inspirational ideas. Having the right attitude. "What Is" verses. A rewarding type of work.

6. Be a Kid Again . . . Juvenile Cards 75
by Florence F. Bradley

Why write juveniles? Two basic types—verse cards and activity cards. Using clever rhyme, meter, and wordplay. Me-to-you message. Examples of verse cards. Getting ideas for activity cards. Illustrating. Juvenile age groups. Examples of activity cards. The child-to-adult market.

7. Light and Bright . . . Informals 93
by Dick Lorenz

Situation cards. Defining informals. Whimsicals. Sentimentals. Religious. Sophisticated. Prose and couplets. Origin of informals. Don't forget the purpose—message bearers.

8. Writing for the Humorous Market 99
by Larry Sandman

Many write studio—few write humorous. Humorous vs. studio cards. Illustrated cards. Humorous formats. Short prose. Couplets. Four-lines. Eight-lines—illustrated verse. Parodies. Signs, badges, and certificates. Photo tie-ins. Mechanical pop-ups. Sliders. Die-cut cards. Study market for formats.

Being fresh and original. Clean and neat submissions. The sympathy angle. Patience, patience. Plagiarism.

Greeting Card Writing . . . Starting at the Beginning

by Larry Sandman

It usually starts with a compliment: "You know, you're really talented. You ought to send your ideas to a greeting card company."

You graciously brush the compliment aside. Aunt Agnes is *always* saying nice things like that. But Uncle Ralph concurs: "You should be making money off of this stuff, instead of wasting it on old folks like us."

You really hadn't thought that much about the card you'd written for your aunt and uncle. At first, it was the answer to an emergency. You'd forgotten about their anniversary and didn't have a card. (Geez, you *always* sent Aunt Agnes and Uncle Ralph an anniversary card!) So, on a whim, you decided to sit down and write one yourself, and with surprisingly little effort you composed a little card that was just "perfect" for them.

You knew they'd like it, but you didn't expect them to be so enthusiastic about it that they'd suggest that you send it to a card company. At first, such an idea sounded crazy. But the more you thought about it, the better it sounded, and the next thing you knew, you were back at your desk scrawling your little gem on a sheet of notebook paper, and sending it off to the president of Blue Skies Greetings.

Any ring of familiarity in this? If you say *no,* pat yourself on the back. If you say *yes,* don't feel bad—that's the way most of us make our first contact with the world of greeting cards. The names may change, and the relationships will vary. (Maybe it was a friend instead of an aunt and uncle.) But the plot is generally the same. Somebody recognizes our talent and calls it to our attention. We balk at first, but gradually we're coaxed (some of us more easily than others) into trying our luck in the market. Some of us get lucky. Our idea makes it from the company president's desk to an unusually nice editor who generously attaches a note to our first rejection slip, suggesting that we read a certain book about how to write greeting cards, and that we go to a few card stores and look at the anniversary cards that are being sold there. The editor wishes us luck on our next submission.

Our natural reaction to rejection is disappointment. Maybe even a touch of anger. Who is that editor, anyway? He obviously doesn't know a good card idea when he sees it! After a while our anger subsides, and our disappointment mellows. We say to ourselves "At least the editor was nice enough to answer." And soon we're thinking that maybe it wouldn't hurt to take the editor's advice—to read the "how to" book and to go out and study the market.

Encouraged by the editor's "good wishes" for our next submission, we head out to buy the book and read the cards. Without knowing it, we've taken the first positive step toward becoming successful greeting card writers—we've gone back and started at the beginning!

If there's one mistake that is made by most greeting card writers just starting out, it's that of not starting at the beginning. In our hurry to be discovered by greeting card editors we tend to jump blindly into the water. Some of us drown and some of us manage, with an editor's help, to struggle back to shore. The quick learners among us decide to learn how to swim before jumping in again. The rest just keep jumping in.

As in all fields of writing, there are right ways and wrong ways to go about submitting ideas. You wouldn't submit a novel written on the side of the box your lawnmower came in, but as a greeting card editor I've had the equivalent sent to me: I've gotten greeting card ideas written on the inside of candy bar wrappers, in the margins of a page of newspaper print, and on filthy paper, blotched with stains from coffee and who knows what! I've also received neat, meticulously typed and spaced submissions in which the ideas were no more appropriate for greeting cards than a screen door for a submarine. In all of these cases my advice to the writer is the same: Go back to the beginning; read the texts and study the market.

Since you've stayed with me this far, I'll take it on faith that you're going to read this text. The next step, then, is to study the market. How do you do that? You study the market by spending some time at the card counters of every type of card-carrying store around, from drugstore, to grocery, to specialty shop. Look over the cards and become familiar with what's there. Ask yourself questions about them. How many *birthday* cards are there? How many *get wells?* How many *congratulations on going another whole week without a blowout* cards?

Look at the sentiments. What do the cards really say? Do they all say the same thing, or are there different messages on different birthday cards? How many are rhymed? How many are in prose? What words or phrases appear over and over? What words that you would expect to find do not appear? As you go from store to store, try to notice any differences among the cards that different companies put out. There are countless questions you can ask yourself. At first the task might seem impossible, the numbers of cards overwhelming. But each time you go out you'll discover more and more about the field.

As you buy cards to send, analyze them. Ask yourself why you bought the card you did. Why did you put back the others? Why did it seem fitting for the person you chose it for? And when you receive cards, ask yourself why each particular card was especially appropriate to be sent to you, or, at least, why the sender might have chosen this card for you.

You can also learn a lot by listening to the conversations of people who are buying cards. What do they think is cute, or clever, or funny, or stupid?

Don't think of market study as a project that you spend one whole day on, then decide you're done. Take your time—shop casually. There's nothing to rush to except rejection slips. You want to find out as much as you can about the market *before* you start submitting. And once you have begun selling card ideas, you'll want to continue to study the market. It doesn't matter if you've been in the business for thirty days or thirty years—you can still learn more about greeting cards every time you walk up to a counter.

You would be surprised at how many "writers" who have been

submitting ideas for a long time still do not really know what a greeting card is. According to my dictionary, a greeting is a "salutation at meeting; a compliment from one absent." In greeting card terms the word greeting means simply "a me-to-you message."

Remember those four words: *me-to-you message.* They will be repeated over and over again in this book because they're the four most important words you'll ever hear in this business. If you keep them in mind as you write your greeting cards, you'll be off and running toward success. If you forget them, you'll be off and crawling . . . back to the beginning.

Now let's get into the different types of greeting cards being made today. Keep an open mind. I have talked to numerous freelancers who claim that they owe their success in greeting card writing to versatility. They feel that to limit oneself to a particular form of greeting card writing is akin to walking the high wire without a net. Don't get me wrong; I'm not saying that you can't make it as a specialist. Several writers have done well specializing in one area like inspirational verse or studio gags. I'm just saying that if you have the talent to do it, you should branch out. You know—"Don't put all your gags in one basket." There's no great risk of spreading yourself too thin. There are only six or seven different types of cards being made, and even these categories do a lot of overlapping. The sentiment "Hope your birthday's wonderful . . . just like you!" could appear on a conventional card or on an informal, a humorous, a studio, a personal relationship, or even on a juvenile card of the proper age group. The idea is flexible enough to be illustrated with any type of art.

The types of cards listed above, along with inspirationals, make up the entire gamut of greeting cards today. Each type can be broken down into different varieties, or any of the types can appear in a special promotion—which we'll discuss later—but the basic types of greeting cards are all listed here. Next we're going to consider each type separately. Some have more than one name. Don't worry too much about names right off—they'll come to you naturally with time. Just try to follow the general idea of what each type is about. Each has at least one full chapter devoted to it later.

Conventional cards, sometimes called **general** (though I prefer to use that word to mean anything that isn't specific), are the "cash cards" of the industry. They're our meat and potatoes, the sentiments that put food in our bellies and fuel in our cars. They are the verses that sell well enough and consistently enough to allow us the luxury of taking chances with the others.

Conventional cards carry a serious (as opposed to a cute or funny) message. They can be written in rhymed verse or prose, varying in length from a few words to twelve or sixteen lines. The most common are short prose, and four-line and eight-line rhymed verses. The message itself may be a rather formal "Happy Birthday, and best wishes for the coming year," or a very warm thought like this one from a valentine for Mother and Dad:

> There's an often-used expression
>   that no matter where you roam
> You'll never find another place
>   that's quite the same as home . . .
> And though the years may change some things
>   these words will still hold true
> As long as there are parents
>   warm and wonderful as you!

Personal relationship cards are an extension of conventional prose. Somewhere between being poetic and being conversational in tone, they are an attempt to put serious, warm, and loving thoughts into a more contemporary sound. Most personal relationship cards are designed with photographs or paintings of romantic settings, nature settings, or landscapes, with short prose sentiments like "wherever you are . . . is where my heart calls home."

Inspirational cards are also an offshoot of conventional cards. Once a slightly poetic, religious-sounding part of the conventional line, these long rhymed verses came into their own with the tremendously successful works of Helen Farries at Buzza Cardoza and Helen Steiner Rice at Gibson. Today most of the major companies carry separate inspirational lines or promotions, and the inspirational verse is becoming more and more recognized as an entity.

Outstanding inspirational verse is eagerly sought by editors because it is not easy to find. There is a fine line between a good inspirational verse that can elevate your spirits and a bad one that sounds overly dramatic and terribly corny. It takes special talent to walk the line and come out with a truly inspirational verse. Here's an example of an inspirational classic by Helen Steiner Rice:

Climb Till Your Dream Comes True

Often your tasks will be many,
And more than you think you can do . . .
Often the road will be rugged,
And the hills insurmountable, too . . .
But always remember, the hills ahead
Are never as steep as they seem,
And with faith in your heart start upward
And climb till you reach your dream,
For nothing in life that is worthy
Is ever too hard to achieve
If you have the courage to try it
And you have the faith to believe . . .
For faith is a force that is greater
Than knowledge or power or skill,
And many defeats turn to triumph
If you trust in God's wisdom and will . . .
For faith is a mover of mountains,
There's nothing that God cannot do,
So start out today with faith in your heart
And "Climb Till Your Dream Comes True"!

Juvenile cards are written to be sent *to children* or *by children*. There are two kinds of juvenile cards—verse cards and activity cards. Verse cards are juvenile versions of conventional cards. They carry a direct me-to-you message from the sender to the receiver, spiced up with pleasant rhymes, bright meters, and funny wordplays. Activity cards are cards that include a game, puzzle, story, or some other plaything. Juvenile cards pay fairly well but the market is limited for the most part to a few of the major companies.

One thing to keep in mind when doing juvenile activity cards is the cost of producing the card. Fresh, new ideas for activities are welcome, but if the idea calls for something too elaborate it might make the card too expensive to produce. Here is a juvenile activity card that would be relatively inexpensive to make:

Hi there! Merry Christmas!

No need to wait till Christmas,
Start having fun right now.
Play Santa's brand-new *bingo* game,
Inside tells you how . . .

[*Inside the card is a spinner and a bingo game that uses toys instead of numbers.*]

Informal cards, sometimes called **cutes**, are a recent development, having grown out of a recognized need for something lighter than conventional cards but not as harsh as studio. Ironically, informals have done so well since their introduction in the early 1960s that shock waves have been felt in the studio line, where soft, cute sentiments are being filtered in with much success. Informal cards often use plays on words or soft humor, and they are usually designed so that the art and editorial tie in with one another. For example:

[*cute toy horse on cover*]

Forget your birthday? . . .
. . . NEIGH! Have a happy!

Humorous cards, like juveniles, can be simple me-to-you messages, or cards with mechanicals, games, puzzles, or some other kind of "play value." Humorous cards are sometimes called *illustrated* cards because there is almost always a strong tie between the sentiment and the art. Humorous cards come in all shapes and sizes, using all types of editorial approaches—prose, short rhyme, or long rhymed verse. Here's an example of a typical long rhymed verse in which each image is illustrated separately with its own humorous rendering:

About Birthdays

They have 'em down in AFRICA . . .
And in the POLAR REGION . . .
They have 'em on the DESERT
(Even in the FOREIGN LEGION . . .)
They have 'em in the MOUNTAINS . . .
They have 'em on the WATER . . .
They may not have 'em up on MARS,
But, anyway, they oughter . . .
They have 'em almost EVERYWHERE . . .
But NOWHERE ELSE, it's true,
Could there be a HAPPIER BIRTHDAY
Than the one that's wished for YOU!

Studio cards are the thigh slappers of the industry. While humorous cards are meant to tickle you, studios are meant to make you double over with laughter. They're the black sheep of the greeting card family, the cards that weren't supposed to stick around. No one ever thought that the little, makeshift departments staffed by people who laughed at their belly buttons would ever stand a chance of making money. But they did. And now, nearly three decades after the time when no self-respecting company would even admit to making studio cards, everyone is proud and happy to lay claim to their birth.

One of the reasons for the great success of studio cards has been their ability to keep up with the times. Studio cards thrive on contemporary humor—the topics and the styles that people are laughing at now. So it stands to reason that the humor in studio cards is constantly changing. What was topical and funny in the 1970s may not be funny today, and what we laugh at today may not be considered funny tomorrow. Of course that's good news for writers, because it means that there will always be a need for new, fresh ideas for the studio line.

That's not to say that nothing lasts in humor. Some gags have a sort of timelessness to them. They are gags about things that can be rediscovered by each upcoming generation—things like belly buttons! Nobody tells us about our belly buttons. We have to learn about them ourselves, somewhere out on the streets. They don't write them up in textbooks—we learn on our own . . . with our friends. And that's what makes them exciting! It's what keeps generation after generation coming back to studio gags the likes of:

[*outside*]   Have fun on your Birthday,
              but don't drink too much beer!!

[*inside*]   I know a guy who did that
              and he blew out his belly button!
              HAPPY BIRTHDAY!

In addition to all of the basic types of greeting cards we've just touched upon, most of the major companies publish independent groups of cards on a single theme, called **promotions**. Promotions can be made up of cards from any of the basic types. They can all be humorous. They can all be inspirational. They can all be personal relationship cards. What sets them apart is that they all share a common theme, such as spring flowers, or seascapes, or the circus. All of the cards in a promotion are designed around the theme, and all of the sentiments are selected to be compatible with that theme.

The purpose of a promotion is to bring in *plus business,* business over and above what the counter lines alone would bring in. And to do that, promotions must depend on *impulse* purchases. They have to have a strong appeal so that a customer might look at them and say, "I just *have* to buy this one for my sister! And I simply *must* get this one for Mom! And look at this one—it has Aunt Agnes written all over it!"

Needless to say, trying to write cards that have that much appeal (especially twelve or more of them) is a real challenge for any greeting card writer.

Now that we've seen what types of cards to write, let's see what happens to your ideas when you send them in to a greeting card company.

You begin with a blank piece of paper. You sit there staring at it for a while, hoping that something will somehow miraculously appear on the page. When nothing happens you begin to wonder if maybe you weren't cut out for this kind of writing. But deep down you know you can do it, so you force yourself to write. You think of the category you want to write for, then a caption and a theme. But this is just to help you get started. If your thoughts lead you to another caption or another theme, you go along. In your mind you wrestle with the different techniques and methods of writing that you have learned. Suddenly something clicks. You have an idea. You hurriedly scribble it down. Oh, it's rough still. But you know there's something there. So you work on it, shorten it, tighten it up. In time it is polished and you can put it aside until you have created its companions who will share an envelope and a batch number on their journey to the greeting card company.

Once you've gotten enough ideas together, given them one final polishing, coded them up, and made copies for your records, you're ready to send them off. You try to put them out of your mind after they're gone—try not to think about how many days or weeks they've been out. But you can't help but wonder about them— about how that cold, uncaring editor is treating your precious brainchildren. Then, just about the time you begin to suspect that the editor has taken all your ideas and stolen off to Mexico, your submission returns. Instantly you will find out if the editor is a hero or a jerk. And today . . . he's a hero!

The editor has sent back all but one of your ideas, and in place of that idea is a note that says, "Thanks for sending in your ideas. I am buying idea #B-WIH for $50. Your check should arrive within two weeks." And just like that your world brightens up. You love your editor and your mailman. Tomorrow you might hate them both, but that doesn't matter now. Today you're ready to sit down at the typewriter and face a whole ream of blank pages. Today you're a professional writer and you know it!

And what about that idea you sold? the one that you pulled,

prayed, and perspired into existence? the one you revised, rewrote, polished, and repolished until you had created a sparkling gem that no editor could be too blind to see? What will become of that?

Having been purchased, it will already have come into the editorial department, been sorted by a clerk and distributed to the proper editor. In many companies it will have been screened for the editor by someone who is trained to do that—someone who has a good knowledge of what the editor needs and doesn't need. Since the assistant who screens mail is intelligent, he has passed your idea along to the editor. Oh, what a day it's been for the editor! Deadlines to meet, sentiments to review, assignments to make for staffers, phone calls to return, and everything is top priority. And on top of it all there's the mail! The editor grumbles as he picks up today's stack. Yours just happens to be on top. He pulls your ideas out of the envelope, and mechanically rejects the first two. But when he reaches the third idea he stops. Slowly a smile starts to work its way up his neck and onto his face. You've sent him a gem and he knows it.

The editor doesn't find any more ideas in your group that stand out like that one, but he doesn't mind. He puts your batch in a special place and holds onto it until he can take it to a freelance mail review meeting. It's there that he might try to sell an idea to his associates. This time the idea sells itself. Everybody likes it and the editor is given the go-ahead to buy it.

Once the editor has given you notice of his intention to buy the idea, he either finds an immediate place for it in his lines, or banks it until an opening occurs. If the idea is really different, he might send it on to marketing research to have it consumer-tested with many other sentiments. Naturally this idea tests well, and the editor, finding an immediate opening for it, sends it on to the art director.

The art director then assigns a staff or freelance artist to create a design to accompany your sentiment. The artist will make one or more rough concepts to take back to the art director. If the art director likes a concept, it is sent to a concept review meeting that is attended by the art director, the artist, the editor, a line planner, the creative director, and perhaps an executive or two. If the concept is approved, it goes back to the artist to be rendered into finished art. Once completed and approved at a finished art review, the design and sentiment are turned over to the lettering department, where your message actually becomes a part of the card. Then there's a final check by art director and editor before the card goes on to platemaking, where the printing plates are created. Then the plates are sent to the printing department where they're set up on a press.

Perhaps twenty thousand cards are printed with your idea. Then they're sent on to the finishing department where any special kinds of die-cuts or finishes are added. Then they're folded, packed, and stored to await shipment.

But before a card can be shipped, it has to be sold. So a certain number of cards are left with the sampling department, who organize them into sample kits and send them to the salesmen out in the field. The salesmen immediately start showing their new samples to store owners and buyers, who then place their orders for the new cards. In time the first orders are on their way to several hundred stores across the country. Your card is among them.

Shortly after your card arrives in the first store, a card clerk puts it in the rack for customers to see. And within hours of the time it goes on display, your card is picked up by a customer who exclaims, "This one is just perfect for Aunt Agnes!" So the customer takes it to the counter, pays for it, takes it home, and mails it to Aunt Agnes. A couple of days later, some five hundred miles away, Aunt Agnes is going to have her day brightened.

In all, it's been about a year and a half since you first submitted your idea—that same idea you pulled, prayed, and perspired into existence; that idea which once was nothing more than a blank sheet of paper and a wish for a miracle.

Your idea has come a long way in its year and a half. Through the medium of greeting cards, you, a writer, have reached out from your desk and touched other people—reached out and made people happy. It makes you think, doesn't it?

Maybe Aunt Agnes and Uncle Ralph were right . . . maybe you *do* have a special gift . . .

Conventional Verse . . . The Heart of the Industry

by Laurie Kohl

If you're new to greeting card writing, you may be a little bewildered by some of the terminology used in the industry.

Conventional is usually defined in dictionaries as "adhering to established form or custom," but in greeting card language it's more easily defined by what it is *not: conventional* refers to rhymed verse or prose that is not humorous, studio, juvenile, cute, or inspirational. The dividing lines among these is not always exact, but conventional verse is the type of verse that makes up the bulk of the lines, everyday and seasonal, of the major greeting card companies. While we use the term *verse* for both rhymed verse and prose, this chapter will deal particularly with rhymed verse.

Conventional verses are, first and foremost, *me-to-you* messages. They are not poetry, outlets for writers' self-expressions, or sermons; they are messages written so that they seem to have been created especially for you, the card customer, to send to the person you have in mind—but they're actually written so that many thousands of people can identify with them and buy them because they say what these people want to say. Conventional verses may carry greetings, expressions of good wishes, congratulations, affection, love, friendship, gratitude, sympathy—or a combination of these.

Probably the first mistake made by beginners in greeting card writing is that their verses are not really greeting cards. Editors receive a constant flow of verses lamenting a lost love, describing a lovely sunset, preaching a religion, reminiscing about the good old days, or even talking to a deceased loved one! Obviously, none of these sentiments are suitable for greeting cards that thousands of people will want to buy and send.

A greeting card verse must fulfill many requirements, but these are the main ones:

1. *It must express the feeling or mood of the occasion or sending situation.* A birthday card, for example, should have a "birthday feeling." A birthday might be a time of memories, a time of looking

forward to the future, a time to celebrate, a time for telling someone how much they're loved or appreciated. But, along with any mention of these, the purpose of a birthday card is to wish someone a happy birthday, so this should always be an integral part of the message. Likewise, a Christmas card should have something of the mood or feeling of Christmas in it.

2. *It must express the relationship of the sender to the recipient.* Since these relationships will vary, so will the types of verses. Some will be formal; some will be simple good wishes, suitable for casual friends, business relationships, or relatives not particularly close to the senders. Others will be warmer, and may include compliments or expressions of affection. These would be suitable for closer friends, or relatives. Some will be romantic, for sweethearts, husbands or wives. Within each of these categories there will be a variety of tone—some will be very light, others more serious. A greeting card company must produce cards of many types, so that a customer coming into the store will be able to find some sentiment that's "just right" for the person he or she has in mind.

3. *It must be upbeat and positive.* Writers tend to have more problems with this when writing humorous cards, but even in conventional cards, dwelling on the negative is something to be wary of. We all realize that close relationships involve bad times, tears, etc., but the more you can avoid negative words and emphasize the positive, the better the feeling left with the reader at the end of the message. After all, the purpose of a greeting card is to try to make someone feel better or happier in some way! For the same reason, avoid being preachy or bossy—Wouldn't you rather be greeted with a smile than with an order or some pious advice?

4. *It must be sendable by many people, to many people.* For this reason, most verses should avoid the use of "I," "me," or "my." It's harder to do, but a verse that can be sent by either one person or by a couple has a much better chance of being bought by an editor, because it also has a much better chance of being bought at the greeting card counter! This limitation, of course, does not apply to the obvious one-to-one relationships such as sweetheart, darling, husband or wife. But it does apply to most relatives. A birthday

verse for mother, ideally, would be sendable by one person or by a couple; would be suitable whether mother lives next door or across the country; whether the sender is a teenager and mother is 35, or the senders are a couple in their fifties and mother is 75; whether mother has you over for dinner every Sunday and babysits for you, or is confined to a nursing home and is not able to do things for you any more; whether she raised you, or is your mother-in-law or your father's second (or third, etc.) wife! Think about all the possible situations and check your verses for limitations; this is what the editors will do, and a verse limited to only one of these kinds of situations is not likely to be purchased.

All these requirements are background for you as you come to the question of what you're going to say in your verse. The best way to get a feel for this is to study the greeting cards you see in the stores. Many aspiring writers will go out and look at a few cards, decide they can do much better, and proceed to try to revolutionize the industry. It won't work. The cards you see in the stores, from the major greeting card companies, are the results of years of research, testing, and analysis; they're the kinds of cards that people buy. You need to shop the card shops, supermarkets, drug, discount, and department stores to see the variety of cards and analyze them. Reduce a long verse to its simplest terms, its message. Just what is it saying? What is the tone of the verse—light and happy? serious? warm and affectionate? How much sentiment is expressed or implied, and how much emotion do you feel when you read the verse? While you're there in the store, notice the customers. These are the people you're writing for. If you're lucky enough to find people shopping together and commenting to each other as they read the verses, do a little eavesdropping. You'll learn a lot—and it's fun! Later, when you get to work on writing verses, try to put yourself in those people's shoes—in a sense, you're ghostwriting for them.

In general, you'll find that cards can be grouped by themes according to the types of messages they convey. Themes include thinking of you, thankful for you, wishing you happiness, you're liked or loved, congratulating you, missing you, hoping for you, sympathizing with you, appreciating you, remembering you, thinking how nice or how special you are, etc. Notice that all these include "you"—and that's no coincidence! "You" is the person who will eventually receive the verse you're going to write, and "you" is the most important word in greeting cards.

As a greeting card writer, you'll be making many trips to the stores to find the answers to the questions you'll have. One of these concerns the different categories, or purpose groups, of the cards. You'll find variations, and changes are made all the time, but these are the major categories you'll find:

EVERYDAY

Birthday, General

Here you'll find a wide range of ideas, moods, and styles—light and serious, short and long, straightforward and affectionate. These are for all ages and types of people, and many are sent to relatives even though they aren't captioned that way. Notice that most of the verses can be sent by either one person or more than one.

Birthday, Specific

Sweetheart, Darling, One I Love: This is the place for those "I" verses! These should be sendable by young or old, married or single, living together or apart. They range from light to very romantic or serious. The "Honey" category is sometimes used in the same way, but in some cases a "Honey" verse is also suitable for a daughter, niece, or granddaughter, so those should not be "I" verses.

From Both, Our Wishes, From All of Us: Since these are from more than one person, they shouldn't be too warm—some of the senders may not be that close to the person. These verses use "we" and "our," and should include the words "both" or "all" in the appropriate categories.

Special Friend: This is a surprisingly large category. Verses are warm, either light or serious, and include the word "friend" or "friendship." Some should avoid saying "I."

Belated: These may include a brief mention of the lateness of the card, but don't dwell on that; emphasize the good wishes for the year ahead. Avoid saying "I." Remember that some cards are belated because the sender was not aware of the recipient's birthday ahead of time; others because the sender procrastinated or just forgot.

Religious: May mention prayers, blessings, God's love and care, but avoid being too heavy or preachy; religious messages should still include a warm feeling toward the recipient. Some religious cards have Bible verses with messages tied in to them. If you use a Bible verse, always give the source (chapter and verse) and indicate which translation of the Bible you're using.

Birthday, Family

This is the largest group of birthday cards, and includes *Mother, Mom, Father, Dad, Sister, Brother, Son, Our Son, Daughter, Our Daughter, Husband, Wife, Aunt, Uncle, Grandmother, Grandma, Grandfather, Grandpa, Granddaughter, Grandson, Son-in-law, Daughter-in-law, Sister-in-law, Brother-in-law, Niece, Nephew, and Cousin.* For all of these, except Husband and Wife, avoid "I" verses. For Our Daughter, and Our Son, use "we" and "our" in your verses. The range of sentiment is wide in the family captions; keep in mind that while some people have close relationships with these relatives, others do not, and so some should simply be warm messages. Try to include mention of the relationship (sister, cousin, etc.) in the verse; if that isn't possible, words like "family" and "relative" are appropriate.

Illness, General

Most illness cards are general, since there are no family captions here. Avoid "I" verses. Also avoid using the words "sick" or "ill" if you can, especially as the rhyming words, where they are emphasized. Be as positive as possible. Remember that some illnesses can be expected to last a while, and so not all these verses should emphasize getting well quickly, or feeling good as new. Try to avoid the temptation to give advice; concentrate on wishes instead. Compliments are good, too, along the lines of "you're too nice to be sick."

Illness, Specific

Hospital: These can be light to serious; people are in the hospital for a variety of reasons, including observation, operations, accidents, childbirth, convalescence. Since some will be there for a long time, not all verses should wish for the patient to get out soon. Try to include something that refers to a hospital, so that the verse is different from a general illness verse. Avoid "I" verses.

Accident: Again, these can be light to serious, as accidents are of all kinds. Avoid "I" verses.

Operation: Light or serious, and avoid the "good as new" phrase—after many kinds of operations, the patient will never be as good as new again. Avoid "I" verses, since this is a small category.

Cheer: This is a larger group of cards, intended for people who may not be expected to recover—the chronically ill or handicapped, people with mental or emotional illness, or having temporary personal or family problems. Don't wish for them to "get well," but say you're thinking of them, hoping they're feeling better, or having a good day. A few can be "I" verses, but you'll have a better chance with a good verse that avoids the "I."

Friendship

Since these are for no particular occasion, they are usually limited to appreciation of friendship, compliments, Hi, Hello, thinking of you, and missing you. This is a fairly small category because most of the major card companies have special groups of promotions which include mostly friendship cards.

Wedding

These are mostly general; only the largest companies have cards for relatives' weddings. Avoid "I" verses. Verses should express good wishes and congratulations, and sometimes warm feelings; but keep in mind that often one of the senders does not know the couple, and a sender who knows one of the couple may not know the other. Keep in mind, too, changing lifestyles. There are now many more second and third marriages, older couples marrying, and couples who have been living together. While none of the verses should be limited to these situations, not all verses should assume a starry-eyed young bride!

Anniversary, General

This is not intended for a wedding anniversary, although it may be used that way. No reference is made to marriage; the card may be used for business anniversaries, or the anniversaries of any personal special occasion, and should be written for either one or more than one recipient. No "I" verses; this is a fairly small category.

Wedding Anniversary, General

This is a large category of cards sent to couples on their wedding anniversaries. Can be light or serious. Some couples may have been married a short time, others for many years; and this may be a second or third marriage. Avoid dwelling too much on the couple's love for each other; concentrate instead on the relationship of the sender(s) to the recipients—wishes for happiness, etc.

Wedding Anniversary, Specific

Our Wishes, From Both: Same as above, remembering that one or more of the senders may not know the couple well. Use "we" and "our."

First Anniversary: A small category, for the couple's first wedding anniversary mention "first" in the verse.

Religious: May mention God, blessings, prayer, etc., but not too heavy on the religion; try to be warm, too!

25th and 50th: Sent to friends or relatives. Avoid "I" verses. Include the words "silver" or "golden," and avoid reference to an idyllic marriage; maybe it isn't! Memories are good as a theme.

Wedding Anniversary, Family

Our Anniversary: These should be equally sendable by wife to husband or husband to wife. Suitable for young or older couples, married a short time or for many years, very much in love or less romantic. Use "I" on these verses!

Wife, Husband: Same as "Our Anniversary," but each is definitely from wife or husband.

Mother and Dad, Mother and Father: Sent by child or children, married or unmarried, to parents. No "I." Since it may be from a couple, or one of the parents may not be the one who raised the sender, avoid specific references to limited situations.

Son and Wife, Daughter and Husband, Brother and Wife, Sister and Husband: May be sent by one person or a couple. These relationships may be close, or not so close. Avoid anything too limiting.

Birth Congratulations, General

Suitable for either a boy or a girl, and for the first baby or the umpteenth! Since these should be sendable by unmarried or non-parent friends, avoid verses that tell the parents what it's like to have a baby! (Also avoid the stork.)

Birth Congratulations, Specific

Boy or Girl: These should be written more specifically with he and him, she and her in the verse. While many of the top-selling verses in the past have emphasized sexual stereotypes, many of the newer verses are careful to avoid these.

Religious, and Christening: Blessings, prayers, God are mentioned; but include some warmth in your verses.

New Grandchild: Small category, published only by a few major companies. Suitable to be sent to either one or two grandparents. Don't assume it's a first grandchild.

Sympathy, General

These are usually short, often prose, expressions of caring. They should not be too heavy on the grief theme.

Sympathy, Specific

Loss of Loved One, Loss of Mother or Father: Mention these specifics within the verse; they should be distinguishable from the general sympathy verses.

From Both, From All, Our Sympathy: Same as above.

Religious: Mention God, prayer, bless, the next life, etc.

Thank You, General

Should be suitable for anything—a gift, kindness, visit. No "I."

Thank You, Specific

Thank You, for Kindness, Flowers, Hospitality, Gift, etc.: Each of these should be specific in the verse as to what the thanks are for. No "I."

From Both, From All, Our Thanks: Use "both," "all," and "we" or "our" in the verse; otherwise, same as general thank you.

Confirmation, First Communion, Bar Mitzvah, Bat Mitzvah

These are all religious occasions and should reflect that, but should also have the appropriate warmth.

Congratulations, Retirement, Travel, Gift, Wishing Success

These and several other small categories can be found in the everyday line of most major companies. Since these categories are often overlooked by freelancers, they can be good categories to write for, and they are worth studying at the counter of your local store.

SEASONAL

Christmas

This is usually the largest seasonal line. It includes many generals, varying from light to serious, formal to warm to sentimental. Generals are sent to friends, relatives, and co-workers. Verses often include the various symbols associated with Christmas. There are numerous family categories for Christmas—all those listed for birthdays, plus the "double relatives" such as son and wife, daughter and husband, etc. There are also many specific categories such as across the miles, from our house to yours, nice neighbors, from both, to both, our wishes, sweetheart, honey, darling, to minister, priest, nun, and general religious. New Year cards are usually done in conjunction with Christmas. New Year messages vary from ighthearted to warm, usually bearing wishes for the holiday and the coming year.

Valentine's Day

This is another large season. Cards are sent to friends and relatives, young and old. Themes are compliments, thinking of you, and how much you mean. Categories are general, sweetheart, darling, one I love, honey, to and from both, and all the family captions as for Christmas.

Easter

Again, a wide range of sentiments ranging from light to serious, expressing thoughts, wishes, and compliments. Many references to spring and, of course, many religious captions. Again, all the family captions as for Christmas, and many generals.

St. Patrick's Day

A smaller season, and generally a lighthearted one. Cards are sent to and from Irish and non-Irish people. The tone is usually light and warm.

Mother's Day

This is a large season, and cards include many generals (suitable for any mother) as well as specifics (from both, our wishes, religious), and cards for daughters, sisters, and wives as well as for mother, mom, and our mother. Tone is light to serious and will naturally include many compliments, but should not be gushy.

Father's Day

Much the same as for Mother's Day, for the male counterparts.

Graduation

For the graduates of elementary, junior high, high school, college or trade school, and graduate school. Verses range from light to serious. Besides the generals, there are specifics for young man, sweet girl, nurse, our wishes, from both, sweetheart, love, son, daughter, etc. Some graduates will be continuing their education and others will not, so don't refer to either. Remember, too, that many graduates are older and have already worked, married, etc., so verses should not all assume a young graduate just going out into the world. This is another place to remember to avoid preachiness or bossiness; concentrate on good wishes and warmth rather than advice!

Grandparents' Day

This is one of the newer seasons, and categories are still evolving, but include general, grandmother, grandma, grandfather, grandpa, and combinations. Light to serious, avoiding "I" verses.

Halloween

A very small season for conventional verse; most Halloween cards are juvenile or humorous. General wishes in a light tone.

Thanksgiving

Light to serious, sometimes rather nostalgic. Generals, to and from both, across the miles, religious, and for the closer relatives and double relatives.

When you've studied the categories, analyzed the verses, and taken notes on themes and ideas, you should have gotten some pretty good ideas on what to say and what not to say. Before you even begin to think in terms of rhyme and meter, think of the message. Write down, in simple prose, what you want to say. This will help you avoid meaningless strings of rhymed lines by establishing an underlying construction with a beginning, middle, and end. It will help you keep your verse clear and coherent, progressing logically from one thought to another with your emphasis at the end. Rhyme and meter are, after all, only means to an end. They can make a message more interesting, more emotional, more beautiful—but the first requirement of a greeting card message is to communicate, and rhyme and meter should never get in the way of communication.

When you've decided what you want to say, you're ready to consider how to say it. This brings us to the rhyme-and-meter department. If you intend to write rhymed verse, you'll find a good rhyming dictionary and a reference on poetic meters and construction very helpful. They'll give you ideas you hadn't thought of. However, since many rhyming words don't lend themselves to greeting card use, especially for conventional verse, here is a listing of the most usable rhymes:

Sounds	*Rhymes*
ad	add, dad, glad, had, sad
after	after, laughter
air	care, compare, pair, prayer, share, where, everywhere, there, anywhere
ake	make, take, cake, mistake, break, sake
ame	same, blame, name, aim, claim, came
and	hand, understand, planned, stand
ar	are, far, star
art	heart, start, part, impart (*rarely*)
ast	last, past, passed, fast
ate	great, date, late, state, wait, congratulate, create, hesitate, anticipate, celebrate
ay	day, way, stay, say, may, convey
aze	days, ways, praise
ear	dear, clear, hear, near, sincere, year, cheer
earn	earn, concern, return, learn, turn, yearn

ee	be, me, see
eel	feel, real, conceal, reveal
eem	dream, seem
eet	sweet, complete, beat, meet, repeat, greet
el	tell, well, excel, bell
end	send, friend, end, mend, spend, depend, extend, blend
ent	sent, went, content, meant, extent
est	best, expressed, blessed, guessed, rest, happiest
et	yet, get, forget, met, regret, bet
eze	these, please, ease
I	high, by, buy, sigh, eye, why, fly, I, sky, deny, reply, try
ice	nice, twice, advice
ick	sick, quick, trick, stick
ide	pride, confide, denied, side, abide, hide, guide, tried, bride, stride, tied
ife	life, wife
ile	smile, while, aisle, style
ime	time, rhyme
in	been, in, spin, begin
ind	find, mind, kind, signed
ine	fine, sign, line, mine
ing	bring, thing, sing, spring
irl	girl, whirl, curl

iss	this, kiss, miss, Sis
ite	night, sight, might, delight, light, right
iv	live, give, forgive
ize	surprise, eyes, rise, wise, qualifies
o	go, grow, know, so, show
old	old, told, bold, hold
oo	you, too, to, two, view, new, knew, do, true, who, through
or	more, before, for, store, door
other	other, mother, another, brother
ow	now, somehow, how, bow
own	own, shown, shone, alone
oy	boy, joy, enjoy, toy
um	come, some, from
un	done, son, sun, one, someone, anyone, everyone, fun, begun, run
uv	love, of, above

This is just a partial list, and you'll notice that greeting card verses frequently use the *oo*, *ay*, and *ear* rhymes because such words as *day, way, say, you, do, too, dear, year,* and *sincere* fit well with greeting card messages. Fresh rhyme schemes are always especially welcome, but be sure they're appropriate to the message and not forced or used in desperation because nothing else would fit!

Most verses are written in exact rhymes, but an occasional near rhyme may be acceptable when not used in an emphatic place such as the ending. Feminine rhymes, those in which the first syllable of words or word combinations are stressed, give a nice variety—for example, *knowing* and *showing, cure you* and *assure you.* However, when mixing words with stressed and unstressed syllables, it is important to be wary of rhymes like *say* and *birthday.* In order to make these words rhyme we must mispronounce *birthday,* moving the accent from *birth* to *day.* The result is a word, and consequently a verse, that sounds unnatural. It's a good example of a situation where the rhyme has become more important than the message—a no-no in almost every editor's book.

Most greeting card verses follow this rhyme pattern for four lines: *x a x a* (second and fourth lines rhyming, first and third lines not rhyming). For example:

Wishing you a birthday
That's happy through and through,
For you're so nice, that's just the kind
That you're entitled to!

Eight-line verses usually follow this pattern: *x a x a x b x b* (odd-numbered lines not rhyming, second and fourth lines making one rhyme, sixth and eighth lines making another rhyme). For example:

You're always first within my heart
Within my dreams, as well.
You bring me far more happiness
Than I could hope to tell . . .
And I can't think of anything
That I would rather do
Than share the joys of Christmas time
And all year through with you!

Couplets are used, too, and sets of couplets, rhyming *a a b b* or, if longer, *a a b b c c d d* etc. For example:

Can't let another day go by
Without a special little "Hi"
So you will know without a doubt
That you are being thought about!

Six-line verses can be written in several ways, the most common being two sets of couplets separated by a third rhyme: *a a b c c b*. For example:

Right from the start
   you've been dear to the heart,
      and that's why this birthday card brings
A warm, loving thought
   of each joy that you've brought,
      and a wish for life's happiest things!

Other six-line rhymes could be a standard four-line followed by a couplet *(x a x a b b)* or two sets of three rhyming words *(a a a b b b)*.

Some rhymed verses have patterns that include a line of prose, repeated for emphasis. For example:

For all the ways you show you care—
                  I LOVE YOU . . .
For every moment we share—
                  I LOVE YOU . . .
For the happiness you bring my way,
For all you mean to me each day,
For more than I could ever say . . .
                  I LOVE YOU . . .

Or this one, running a little longer:

A little greeting fondly sent,
A little message warmly meant,
Wishing joy and heart's content . . .
            ESPECIALLY FOR YOU!
A little hope that Easter brings
All its best and brightest things
And lots of pleasant happenings . . .
            ESPECIALLY FOR YOU!
And when the happy hours have fled,
May many good days wait ahead,
And that's a wish that's often said . . .
            ESPECIALLY FOR YOU!

More and more, different patterns are being used, so watch for these as you shop for cards and try them for variety—or create your own! Just be careful that you don't get so tricky that the message becomes lost; your pattern should enhance the message, not overshadow it.

The most frequently used meter in greeting card verse is the *iambic* form that alternates from four metric feet in the odd-numbered lines to three feet in the even-numbered lines. If you remember your lessons in scanning poetry, you know that a foot contains one strong beat, or stressed syllable, and one or more light beats, or unstressed syllables (with the exception of the spondee, in which theoretically there are no unstressed syllables). Reducing it to something like Morse code, the basic iambic 4/3/4/3 verse form goes like this (stressed syllable shown as —, unstressed as ᴗ):

ᴗ —/ᴗ —/ᴗ —/ᴗ —
ᴗ —/ᴗ —/ᴗ —
ᴗ —/ᴗ —/ᴗ —/ᴗ —
ᴗ —/ᴗ —/ᴗ —

Here's a verse that follows the pattern exactly:

A Recipe for Your Birthday, Mom

Just take a happy birthday, Mom,
    and many, many more . . .
Then add to those each happy thing
    that you've been hoping for . . .
Now top it off with best of health
    and happiness each day,
And you'll have every loving wish
    this card has brought your way!

The opposite of iambic is *trochaic,* a foot consisting of an accented syllable followed by an unaccented one:— ᴗ/— ᴗ/— ᴗ/— ᴗ. A verse in this meter would read:

Wishing you a happy birthday,
    filled with joys each minute!

Hoping every day that follows
    has more good things in it!

However, most verses do not follow either pattern exactly. An unaccented syllable is often either omitted or added at the beginning of a line. And, since most rhyming words are accented on the last (or only) syllable, a foot is often cut short, or completed at the beginning of the next line. For example, this verse:

Until You're Well Again

A Rose and a Wish

A rose to say you're thought of
    in a fond and special way,
And a wish that you're much better
    and improving every day,
With all the very best of health
    and happiness in view,
Just the way it ought to be
    for someone nice as you!

The verse would be scanned like this:

ʊ —/ʊ —/ʊ —/ʊ
ʊʊ —/ʊ —/ʊ —
ʊʊ —/ʊ —/ʊ
ʊʊ —/ʊ —/ʊ —
ʊ —/ʊ —/ʊ —/ʊ —
ʊ —/ʊ —/ʊ —
—/ʊ —/ʊ —/ʊ —
ʊ —/ʊ —/ʊ —

This is basically an iambic verse. The extra unaccented beats at the beginnings of lines 2 and 4 are taking the place of accented beats missing at the ends of their preceding lines, and there's an extra beat at the beginning of line 3. There's also an incomplete foot at the beginning of line 7. These variations allow a smooth transition from one thought to another in the verse, yet are minor enough that they do not interfere with readability.

Another useful meter for greeting card verses is *anapestic:* two unaccented syllables followed by an accented one. A typical line would be ᴜᴜ _/ᴜᴜ _/ᴜᴜ _/ᴜᴜ _ as in this verse:

It's a blessing to have
   a grandmother like you;
It's a joy on your birthday
   to think of you, too,
And a pleasure to tell you
   you're specially dear—
May God bless you, Grandmother,
   today and all year!

The reverse of this meter is *dactylic:* _ ᴜᴜ/ _ ᴜᴜ/ _ ᴜᴜ/ _ ᴜᴜ. The last foot is often cut short in rhymed verse:

Everything Christmassy,
Everything bright,
Everything merry
From morning till night—
That's what you're wished
At this time of good cheer,
Along with life's best
Through a wonderful year!

This verse is basically dactylic, with the last foot cut short in the rhymed lines, and with an extra unaccented beat inserted at the beginning of line 7. The addition or omission of a beat in line 7 often serves as a signal that the end of the verse is approaching, and has the effect of adding emphasis to the ending.

The anapestic and dactylic meters tend to give a light, happy feeling or tone to a verse, and most editors would like to see more of them. Sometimes, when you just can't seem to get a verse to come out right in whatever meter you're using, a change to another meter can be the answer. Writers often forget about these more unusual meters and the great potential they hold.

Regardless of the meter you're working with, reading your verses aloud can help you to determine whether or not your words flow smoothly. If you have a good basic sense of rhythm, and have read a lot of greeting card verses, you'll be able to tell when you need to keep your meter exact and when you can vary it slightly to say what you want to say; and you'll also learn to avoid the singsong effect that can come with a long verse in exact meter.

In writing rhymed verse, check yourself for any tendency to force the meter. The accent on a syllable should always fall exactly where it falls in natural speech. Check also for inverted word order, as, for example, "memories sweet" instead of "sweet memories." This is usually done in order to make something fit into a meter or to get a rhyming word, and, while poets can get away with it, greeting card writers can't.

Though we don't naturally talk in rhyme and meter, greeting card verses should always be as *conversational* as possible. Wherever you can, use contractions in your verses. Say "you'll" instead of "you will"—that's the way people talk. Sometimes this will be a help to you in working out your meter, and sometimes it will cause you problems, but always work toward the most natural, conversational expression. Greeting card verses are not the place for stilted or scholarly language.

Some of the language used in verses in the past has become dated or for some other reason inappropriate for use in greeting cards today. Here's a list of some words and phrases to avoid in your verses:

swell and *guy* (sound old)
gay (this used to be a good rhyme word, but current usage gives it quite a different meaning!)
sure hope, sure glad, sure think, etc. (padding)
real (as a substitute for very or really)
just (as in "just every way") (padding)
mighty (as in "mighty nice") (sounds old)
condolences, bereavement (stilted)
chum, pal, glum, feeling blue (sound old)
o'er, e'er, etc. (too poetic, sound old)

Sometimes it's tempting to use some of these words—some of them have the rhyme sounds you want, some will pad out your meter or fill up a line for you. *But a verse that has one weak word or line is an unfinished verse.* You'll need to revise, often many times, to perfect a verse, and sometimes your final verse will be quite different from the one you started out with. Don't fall so much in love with your first version that you can't bear to throw out, dissect, rearrange, or add to it—or even start over—to get it right. It must fulfill all the requirements of meaning, sincerity, naturalness of expression, good rhyme and meter, or it will not be purchased. Add to that the necessity for originality—some little twist or interesting idea or phrasing that sets it apart from the thousands of similar verses—and you can see that greeting card writing is not something that can be done successfully off the top of your head! As a free-lancer, your work must compete with the many verses the card companies already have on file, the work of their staff writers, and the work of all the other freelancers. Attention to all the factors that make a successful verse is what separates the amateur from the professional; and if you're going to be a pro, that's your challenge!

How can you make your verse stand out from all the others? One way is to structure it around a definite *idea*. Ideas for verses can come from many places: ads, slogans, and commercials; songs—old standards, popular, country and western, hymns; current interests and lifestyles—sports, ecology, gardening, book themes. In addition, some of the most popular designs for greeting cards can be used: pansies, roses, gardens, bouquets, wishing wells, and gateways are all designs that have led to successful greeting card verses written around those themes. Try a recipe format. Or write a nice legend based on some symbol used on greeting cards. The possibilities for such special verses are endless, as long as you remember that the verse must contain a me-to-you message, or you must write a brief message that ties in with it.

Quotations are often used along with verses, and, in fact, often inspire the verse. If you use quotations from famous authors, be sure that the quotations are old enough to be in the public domain. *(Editor's Note:* Published works enter the public domain either 50 years after the author's death or, if written for hire, 75 years after publication or 100 years after their creation, whichever is less.) Here is an example of a verse that ties in nicely with a quotation:

[*page 2*]   Friends—they cherish
                   each other's hopes. . .
                       they are kind
                           to each other's dreams.
                                    —Thoreau

[*page 3*]   Birthdays come and birthdays go,
                   but with them comes the thought
               That life is always richer
                   for the things the year has brought,
               And friendship, too, is richer,
                   for each day adds something new
               When the joys of life are shared
                   with such a special friend as you!

With the quote about friends, the verse starts off rather philosophically and ends up with a nice, warm compliment for the "special friend." There's a special thought behind it that makes it different from most verses.

Sympathy verses are hard to write well, but sometimes you can get your message across better in the form of a "quote" that you create:

[*caption*]   *With Sympathy in the Loss*
                   of Your Loved One

[*page 2*]   To live in the hearts
                   of those we leave behind
                       is to live forever.

[*page 3*]   This brings you deepest sympathy
                   and comes to tell you, too,
               You're specially thought of in the loss
                   of one so dear to you.

If the writer had attempted to say in verse what he said in the quote on page 2, it would have sounded preachy. By removing it from the direct message, it's a nice addition to the personal message and says something meaningful and comforting. Don't expect to have your name on the card as the author of your quote, though; most companies have their own special names they like to keep using, or they will simply use quotation marks or a different lettering style to set it apart.

In this wedding card, the writer wanted something suitable for close friends or relatives to send—something that sounded very affectionate, but would not be limited to relatives. Again, a quote sets the tone and says something that would be too limiting if it were said in the verse itself:

[*page 2*]   One of the sweetest
                     joys in life
                        is seeing the happiness
                           of those we love.

[*page 3*]   It's a wonderful,
                    beautiful time in your lives—
                       when your love and your marriage are
                       new,
                 And a wonderful time
                    for the people who love you
                       and want all your dreams to come true;
                 So this comes with a wish
                    that your marriage will always
                       be filled with the things you hold dear,
                 And the joy in your hearts
                    as your married life starts
                       will grow deeper and sweeter each year.

This is really an eight-line verse, with very long lines that are split apart. Whenever you write in long lines, be sure that the lines have good breaking places, because greeting cards, being more vertical than horizontal, can't accommodate long lines.

Another kind of split that's commonly found in greeting cards is that of the *split verse,* a verse that begins on one page and ends on another. Editors are usually looking for verses that split well, as they are often needed for three-fold cards. Such verses must break naturally, with each part being capable of standing alone. Here's an example:

[*page 1*]   *From Our Home to Yours*
                        at Thanksgiving

[*page 2*]   This brings a warm wish
                        and a special wish
                              to those at your address . . .

[*page 3*]   May Thanksgiving
                        find your home and hearts
                        filled with happiness!

The traditional ellipsis, or three dots, indicates that the verse is continued on the following page. You might note that although both parts are needed to make the total verse, each part contains a complete thought of its own. This is typical of split verses. If properly written, a verse can begin on page 1 and continue, with segments, on each subsequent page of the card.

Special verses are frequently needed for the large, more expensive cards. These are usually rhymed verses on page 2, followed by a prose message on page 3. Such titles as "What Is a Mother?" or "Parents Are a Blessing" are examples. Since the me-to-you part of these cards is usually written in prose, these combinations will be covered in the next chapter.

Conventional Prose

by Laurie Kohl

The use of prose in greeting cards has changed and expanded a lot in the past few years. It was once used mainly in the more formal counter cards and boxed Christmas cards, and also in studio, humorous, and cute cards. Now, however, many kinds of prose are used in conventional cards, and used in many ways. There's formal prose, "soft" prose, long prose, used either as the direct message or as a "special verse," and prose sentiments written to tie in with rhymed verse or quotations.

The requirements for prose are basically the same as for rhymed verse—except for the absence of rhyme and meter. Messages must still be upbeat and sendable to many people for the appropriate occasions, sending situations, and relationships. They must still sound as natural and conversational as possible. This doesn't mean that prose can just ramble on aimlessly, though—an underlying construction and logical development are just as important in prose as in rhymed verse; maybe more so, because without the sparkle of interest that rhyme and meter give, prose can quickly become dull. While your greeting card prose, as used in the direct me-to-you message, should be natural and sincere rather than poetic, you can borrow a few ideas from the poets to make it interesting and give it a flowing, melodic quality.

You won't be working in the definite meter patterns of rhymed verse, but prose that *sounds* best usually does have a rhythm to it—a repetition of metric feet here and there, as in this example from a sympathy card:

Only you can really know your loss . . .
        . . . but your sorrow is felt and shared.

If you were to scan this, it would come out:

ᵕᵕ —/ᵕ —/ᵕ —/ᵕ —
ᵕᵕ —/ᵕᵕ —/ᵕ —

This is actually pretty similar to a regular meter as found in rhymed verse. It is written mostly in iambic meter, and only the anapestic feet in the middle keep it within the realm of prose. Most prose isn't this regular, but it should still have some repetition of metric feet to give it coherence and a flowing quality. Reading your prose aloud, just as you would rhymed verse, will help you find the rough spots and see where you need to cut, add, or change for the smoothest sound.

Some of the other characteristics of poetry that can help you in writing prose are *alliteration, consonance,* and *assonance.* These are good in rhymed verse, as well, but in prose you're free of the limitations of fitting into definite metrical patterns and rhyme schemes, so you can make more liberal use of them.

Alliteration, the repetition of the same consonant sound at the beginnings of words, is used frequently in greeting card prose, as in this short cheer verse:

[caption]   *Wishing You Sunnier Days*

[page 3]   Hope everything
             will soon be brighter
             and better for you!

The *b* sound is repeated in *be, brighter,* and *better,* and there's also the repetition of the *t* within the latter two words. The words just seem to belong together, both because of the alliteration and because of their rhythm. Yet none of this is forced; the message is a simple, sincere, appropriate one for anyone having problems.

Here's a slightly longer one:

[page 1]   May your birthday bring you
             all the happiness
                 you could hope for . . .

[page 3]   . . . and may all your tomorrows
             be as happy as today.

Here the *b* is repeated in *birthday* and *bring,* and again in *be* on the inside of the card. The *h* appears in *happiness* and *hope*, and reappears on the inside in *happy*. The *t* in *tomorrows* and *today* not only adds alliteration, but the words themselves are a nice contrast to each other and seem to give just the emphasis you need to wrap it up at the end.

Consonance, the repetition of the pattern of consonants, is not as frequently used as alliteration because there's a limit to the word combinations suitable for greeting card use that share the same consonants, but here's one possibility:

[*caption*]   *Congratulations*
                    on Your Marriage

[*page 3*]   May your life together
                    be filled with love.

While the *f* and *v* sounds aren't exactly alike, *life* and *love* are close enough in their *l* and *f* consonant sounds to make a nice pattern together. *Filled* has the same sounds, in reverse order, and adds to the feeling of completeness.

Assonance, the repetition of vowel sounds, is also less frequent than alliteration, but can be used effectively, as in this example:

[*caption*]   *Get Well Wishes*
                    Just for You

[*page 3*]   Wishing you a good day,
                    cheerful spirits,
                    and a quick recovery!

The same vowel sound appears in *wishing, spirits,* and *quick;* and combined with the repetition of *r,* the rhyming sound of the syllables *cheer* and *spir,* and the three-part pattern (more about that later!), the verse has several things that elevate it above the ordinary. Yet you don't really notice them at first reading. The message—what you're saying—is always the most important thing; never let any gimmick stand out so much that the message gets lost!

Among the types of prose, the oldest and most conventional is formal prose, as, for example:

> Congratulations on your birthday
> and best wishes for the year ahead.

Or:

> Wishing you a Merry Christmas
> and much happiness in the New Year.

These formal sentiments are so standard, and allow for so little variety, that there really is no point in submitting them; the card companies have them in their files and reuse them year after year.

A little less formal would be a simple, straightforward message such as:

[*caption*]   *Wedding Wishes*
                   from All of Us.

[*page 3*]   All of us wish you happiness
                   as you begin your new life together.

Again, a very sendable message, but the editor is likely to have it, or something very similar, already in the files. The very short, simple verses have probably been done many times before. What the editor needs from you, the freelancer, is the kind of conventional prose that takes a little more thought—and more work!

Some of the patterns that can help you in writing prose are *repetition, contrast, three-part,* and *parallel construction.*

The *repetition* of consonant and vowel sounds has already been discussed, but the repetition of words and phrases can also be pleasing. Maybe it's a carryover from our early childhood days, when we wanted the same story read to us over and over again, and we jumped rope endlessly to the same little rhymes. We all seem to like the familiarity that comes with repetition! And it's reflected in the success of greeting card sentiments like this one:

[*caption*]   *For Your Golden*
                     Wedding Anniversary

[*page 3*]　　　　The fifty years you two have shared
　　　　　　are fifty reasons to be happy for you . . .
　　　　　　　fifty reasons for congratulating you . . .
　　　　　　　fifty reasons for wishing you
　　　　　　　the happiest anniversary you've ever
　　　　　　　had!

Repetition can be used to tie a page 3 me-to-you message to a page 2 quotation or special thought, as the next example shows:

[*caption*]　　　　*Congratulations*
　　　　　　on Your Baby!

[*page 2*]　　　　A baby is
　　　　　　one part sunshine,
　　　　　　　two parts fun,
　　　　　　　　three parts love . . .
　　　　　　　　rolled into one!

[*page 3*]　　　　Wishing you
　　　　　　all of the fun
　　　　　　all of the joy
　　　　　　all of the love
　　　　　　　of growing and being together!

The repetition in the following verse is more subtle, but it's there:

[*caption*]　　　　*Congratulations*
　　　　　　as You Graduate from College

[*page 3*]　　　　You have every reason to be proud . . .
　　　　　　and you have everything it takes
　　　　　　　for a bright and happy future!
　　　　　　CONGRATULATIONS AND BEST
　　　　　　WISHES

The opposite of repetition, *contrast,* can also be effective in verses contrasting yesterday, today, and tomorrow; memories and hopes; the past and the future; large and small, as in this verse for a little thank you card:

[*caption*]   *Thank You*
            for Being So Nice
            to Our Baby!

[*page 3*]   This card is small,
            but our thanks
            are "family size" . . .
            THANK YOU!

Three-part patterns have long been popular in rhymed verse, and can be used in different lengths of prose. Here's a verse that uses a three-part repetition of the familiar toast phrasing, "Here's to . . .":

[*caption*]   *As We Celebrate*
            Our Wedding Anniversary
            Here's to our love . . .

[*page 2*]   Here's to our marriage . . .

[*page 3*]   Here's to us!
            HAPPY ANNIVERSARY

The following verse, intended for a masculine birthday card, repeats the pattern of each line in its three parts:

[*caption*]   *Happy Birthday*

[*page 3*]   May this day begin a year
            of new paths to take . . .
            new hills to climb . . .
            new views to enjoy

The following verse also exhibits a three-part repetition, but uses it to build a sense of expectancy that is resolved by the strongly complimentary, warm, but not sentimental page 3 message. This card has a more complex structure than the previous examples, containing secondary repetitions in addition to the major three-part construction:

[caption]   *A Valentine for My Wife*

[page 2]   In the way you live each day with joy,
In the way you touch other people with
warmth,
In the way you fill my life
with happiness and love . . .

[page 3]   I see again and again
that I found a very special woman
when I found you!

Did you notice the consonance (*life—fill—life—love*) and the subtle alliteration (the *ch* in *each* and *touch*, the *th* in *other* and *warmth*)?

Another kind of three-part construction doesn't repeat the same words, but parallel words—in this case, *remembering, thinking,* and *wishing:*

[caption]   *For a Special Friend*
at Christmas

[page 3]   Remembering
the many happy times
we've shared . . .
Thinking
what a specially
good friend you are . . .
Wishing you
a wonderful Christmas
and year ahead!

Again, notice the *sh* sound in *shared* and *specially*, the *d* in *shared, friend,* and *ahead.*

Repetition is also a factor in *parallel construction*, in which phrases play off of one another:

[*caption*]   *A Wish for Your Anniversary*

[*page 3*]   May it be a day
                    of beautiful memories
                        . . . and may it begin a year
                            of beautiful days.
            HAPPY ANNIVERSARY!

Here, the last word, *days,* takes you back to the first line and gives a sense of completeness. The alliteration of *be—beautiful—begin— beautiful,* the repetition of the *y* sound in *day, year,* and *day,* and the rhyme of *may* and *day* all contribute to the effectiveness of the verse.

Here's another with parallel thoughts:

[*caption*]   *For Mother and Dad*
                    on Their Anniversary

[*page 2*]   Wishing you the kind of day
                    you'll always remember
                    with happiness . . .

[*page 3*]   . . . because you're the kind of parents
                    who are always remembered
                    with love.
            HAPPY ANNIVERSARY

Prose that ties in with a quotation was illustrated earlier in the baby verse, in which the words in the quotation were repeated in the message. But the tie-in can also be to the feel of the quotation rather than to the actual word, as in this one:

[*caption*]   *With Love to You, Mother*
                    The Lord
                        that made heaven and earth
                            bless thee.
                                —Psalms 134:3

[*page 3*]   Your love,
              your understanding,
              and your prayers
                have always been an inspiration.
        HAPPY MOTHER'S DAY, MOTHER

Or this one, in which the quotation is quite sentimental and the direct message is lighter, but affectionate, making the card more sendable:

[*caption*]   *With Love, Grandma*
             on Grandparents Day

[*page 2*]   A grandma is someone special . . .
            life is enriched by her caring
              and warmed by her love.

[*page 3*]   Having a grandma like you
            is one of the nicest things
              that could happen to anyone!
        HAPPY GRANDPARENTS' DAY

In this Easter card, the quotation uses "I" but the direct message does not, so the card can still be sent by more than one person:

[*page 1*]   *Mother . . .*
        "If I can see the beauty
        and find the joy
        in every day of life,
        it's because my mother
        first showed me
        where to look"

[*page 3*]   For every lovely thing you've done,
            for every lovely thing you are,
              Bless you, Mother . . .
                at Easter and always!

This figurative, rather than literal, use of the word "I" is called an *editorial I.* It, along with figurative uses of the pronouns "we," "you," and "they," often appear in *special verses*. Special verses are just what the name suggests—verses that are treated differently from regular greeting card verse. Most are titled works, such as "What Is Love?" that are featured on page 1 or page 2 of a card, with an appropriate separate me-to-you message on page 3.

Most special verses are written in rhymed verse, but here's one in prose that could be used appropriately for Valentine's Day or other seasons, as well as for birthday, husband or wife, or sweetheart:

[caption]
> *For Your Birthday, Sweetheart*
> "Why Do I Love You?"

[page 2]
> I love you
> for being
> your own
> special you . . .
> and for
> letting me be
> myself
> I love you
> for overlooking
> and forgiving
> my faults . . .
> and for seeing
> the good in me
> I love you
> for showing me
> the beautiful in life
> and the joy
> in little things
> I love you
> for making me happy
> and for sharing
> my happiness
> I love you
> for all you are . . .

and you are all
the things
I love

[*page 3*]   There must be a million ways
to say "Happy Birthday,"
Sweetheart,
but there's not one
that says it better than this . . .
I love you!

Another combination of a special verse in prose, followed by a
prose direct message, is this one:

[*caption*]   *As You Join Your Hearts in Love*

[*page 2*]   Love begins
like the springtime
with the joy of anticipation,
the promise of dreams coming
true . . .
Love grows
like a summer flower
with warmth and understanding,
with care and affection . . .
Love radiates
with the happiness of fulfillment,
magnificent as a tree
filled with the magic of autumn . . .
Love softens
with a gentle touch
like new fallen snow.

[*page 3*]   Through every season
of your married life,
may your hearts always know
love, joy, and happiness!

The message picks up on the theme of the special verse with the word *season,* tying the two together.

The same thing is done when the special verse is written in rhyme, as in this one:

[*page 1*]   *Count Your Birthdays by Your Memories*

[*page 2*]   Count your birthdays by the memories
                    of the happy years you've spent,
               Count them by each cherished friendship,
                    count them by each glad event,
               Count your birthdays by each happy thing
                    that life has given you,
               And by each joy and pleasure
                    you have brought to others, too . . .
               Count your birthdays by the treasures
                    you have gathered through the years
               And you'll always be delighted
                    as your birthday time appears!

[*page 3*]   Wishing you
                    a memory-making birthday
                    and many, many more!

Since the theme of the special verse is *memories,* the prose picks up on that, adding some more *m* sounds for good measure!

Another special verse is written in a recipe format, and the page 3 message ties in with that by using the word *blend:*

[*caption*]   *A Recipe for a Happy Birthday*

[*page 2*]   Begin with bits of happiness,
               Then add a wish or two . . .
               Combine with special, friendly thoughts
               That last the whole day through . . .
               Then sprinkle in some cheerfulness,
               Add pleasures, one by one . . .

And have a day that's perfect
From the start until it's done!

[*page 3*]   Hope your birthday's
the perfect blend
of all your favorite things!

As you work on any type of prose, think of the way it could best be laid out on a greeting card, because that can make a big difference in the impression it makes. Since lines must usually be short, except on the largest cards, split lines into natural phrases or clauses, and remember that a split between pages 1 and 3, or 2 and 3 should be at a natural break in speech. Sometimes you'll need to type up your verse several different ways to see which looks and reads best, but it's worth the time for the difference it can make. It's just part of all the changing, rearranging, and general "juggling" that makes greeting card writing so complicated . . . and so interesting!

Personal Relationship Cards

by Bernice Gourse

Just as styles in other areas of society change, so do our ways of communicating thoughts and feelings. We seek different ways to express ourselves through new media and through new ways of using traditional media.

As one of the traditional channels of communication, greeting cards have undergone many changes. A demand for conventional greeting card verse has continued through the years, but needs for new ways of expressing thoughts and feelings have brought about such alternatives to conventional verse as studio cards, informals, and, most recently, a type of warm prose sentiments that we call *personal relationship* cards.

Perhaps it has been the unsettled condition of the world that has created a demand for a renewal of an expression of truthfulness, of directness and honesty in personal relationships. Whatever the reasons, a new type of sentiment has gained in popularity in recent years, and "love and affection" has flourished anew in such personal relationship sentiments as these:

[*outside*]   Each time you touch my life . . .

[*inside*]   the sun shines

[*outside*]   When I can't be with you . . .

[*inside*]   I touch you with my thoughts

Greeting card companies have responded to the desire for expressions of deep-seated emotions with personal relationship messages such as "Images" from the Paramount Line, "Tenderness" by Rust Craft, "Soft Touch" by American Greetings, and "Songs of the Earth" from Gibson.

The messages in personal relationship cards are usually short, conversational prose sentiments intended for people who want to communicate intimate personal feelings. They are simple, direct thoughts that reflect warmth and sincerity.

Some of the best selling personal relationship cards in the industry are manufactured by the Paramount Line, whose Images have served as trend setters in this market. Their success has been due in part to their beautiful acetate photographs, and in part to their simple and conversational sentiments that sound genuine, natural, and straightforward:

[*outside*]   I may not understand
                  exactly what you're feeling . . .

[*inside*]   . . . but I care enough
                  to want to share it with you

At Paramount, writers are instructed to imagine themselves in a close, emotional relationship with someone. The caption and verse of each sentiment written should reflect the kinds of thoughts that would occur to two people who are deeply involved, or who share close familial ties, or who are apart and missing one another, or who are sharing a common hurt. By this sort of role playing, writers can create sentiments that express real feelings, feelings with which people who are really in these situations can identify. And, as with all greeting cards, it is this *identification* between card and receiver that sells each personal relationship card. Here is a Paramount card that thousands of people have been able to identify with:

Sometimes our deepest feelings
   are the hardest to express . . .

This could be an expression of sympathy, an apology, or just an expression from the heart to show deep love and affection. As with most good prose, it uses few words to say a lot.

Although in the vast area of human relationships there may be nothing new under the sun, there is always something new to be found in the manner of choosing the right words to express one's innermost feelings. Both of the following sentiments, the first from

Gibson and the second from Paramount, say essentially the same thing—"You're special to me." But their approaches are totally different:

[*outside*]   When I'm with you . . .

[*inside*]   . . . everything's special

[*outside*]   Everyone needs someone
                    who means just a little bit more . . .
                 Someone to sense their moods
                    and understand their needs . . .
                 If they're lucky, someone special
                    comes into their life
                    and enriches it.

[*inside*]   I'm lucky . . .
                    because you are
                 that special someone for me

Personal relationship cards, like all greeting cards, are a means for people to express themselves—to convey good wishes, a compliment, or a special message. Their appeal extends to all age groups and covers a wide range of subjects: birthday, anniversary, friendship, thinking of you, love, sympathy, loneliness, and inspiration. Whether long and romantic, like this Gibson sentiment:

[*outside*]   Our love is for the quiet times . . .

[*inside*]   . . . the festive times,
                 times spent together,
                 times spent apart,
                    serious times,
                       happy times . . .
                 . . . our love is for all times!

or short and pleasant, like this one:

[*outside*]   *On Your Birthday*

[*inside*]   Hope the sun comes up
                   on a happy day for you

they all produce a feeling that the meaning goes much deeper than
the words.

It is this ability to make your words convey a strong message that
will make your material sell. Say something meaningful, touching
on feelings that are universal. If you can do that, if you can find a
new way to say "I care," you will have found the key to success in
personal relationship cards.

Writing
the
Inspirational Verse

by Patricia Ann Emme

The inspirational type of card has been popular for many years, and, no matter how many different types of new card ideas arrive on the scene, the inspirational still stands out as one of the biggest sellers in the card shops.

In 1954 Helen Farries introduced the inspirational card into the Buzza Cardoza line, and for many years she wrote some of the most beautiful inspirational cards in the world.

Helen Steiner Rice, writing for Gibson Greeting Cards, became world renowned for her beautiful inspirationals, which appear not only on cards, but on plaques, stationery, records, and gift items, and in many books as well.

Both these gifted writers knew how to use words to uplift and bring faith and beauty to others by creating beautiful verses which could be used on greeting cards sent for various occasions.

While many conventional cards may also be inspirational in nature, they are generally shorter and their messages are more personal. Their emphasis is on a me-to-you message, delivered more or less directly from the sender(s) to the receiver. Inspirationals tend to be less direct and more poetic. They present beautiful thoughts about life, love, God, and nature in relatively long (compared to conventional) inspiring verses that appeal to a wide audience. Unlike the conventionals, where the me-to-you message rules, and everything else is dressing, inspirationals feature their special verses. In fact, the special inspirational verse often has as much or more to do with selling this type of card than the accompanying me-to-you sentiment. In this respect the inspirational card is set apart from the conventional.

Inspirational greeting cards often bring comfort to someone who is either ill or in bereavement by stressing faith, or God's goodness and mercy, through poetic expression. They are also used to define love as life's dearest gift—making them perfect for weddings and anniversaries.

Inspirational friendship cards are also in great demand, and seasonal cards for Christmas and Easter often carry a long inspirational poem on the front of the card, with a shorter, more conventional verse inside, as in the following:

That's Christmas

The sound of carols in the night,
The golden star that shines so bright,
The glow of Heaven's holy light,
That's Christmas.
The friends who share the special glow,
Of fireside and mistletoe,
The earth alive with glistening snow,
That's Christmas.

On the inside of this particular card the verse reads simply, "Christmas wouldn't be the same without you as a friend."

Or this inspirational Christmas, which was also published by Warner Press:

The Sounds of Christmas

You can hear the sounds of Christmas,
All across this spacious land,
From the hillsides to the mountains,
And above the whistling sands.
You can hear the sounds of Christmas,
On the sidewalks of the street,
And the sound of Christmas laughter,
Comes from happy folks you meet.
Yes, the many sounds of Christmas,
Fill the earth and sky above,
And reflect the joy of Jesus' birth,
And God's perfect care and love!

The inside text on this card reads, "May you all share the many blessings that Christmas time brings."

I sold both of these inspirationals many years ago, but they are still being used today, not only on cards, but in greeting card booklets as well.

The following Easter poem was published by Ideals in one of its Easter booklets, but it could also be used on an Easter card:

Easter

Against a sky of blue and gray,
The dawn of Easter greets the day.
The lilies raise their heads up high,
To kiss the early morning sky.
In bright array upon the hills,
The tulips and the daffodils,
With flaming colors warm and fair,
Tell us God is everywhere!
And that is why the Easter birth,
Brings hope and peace across the earth,
For all things whisper God is true,
As Easter morning comes in view.

As you can see, inspirationals that are seasonal often praise God's gift of nature as well as offer new insight into the meaning of a particular occasion.

Get well cards can also be inspirational and personal, as is this one written by Helen Farries. The poem has appeared on hundreds of cards throughout the years and is still being used today:

I Thought of You and Said a Little Prayer

This morning when I wakened
And saw the sun above,
I softly said, "Good morning, Lord,
Bless everyone I love!"
Right away I thought of you
And said a little prayer,

That He would bless you specially
And keep you free from care . . .
I thought of all the happiness
A day could hold in store,
And wished it all for you because
No one deserves it more!
I felt so warm and good inside,
My heart was all aglow . . .
I know God heard my prayer for you,
He hears them all, you know!

Later on, I wrote something similar for Paramount which appeared on one of their Image cards:

A Prayer for Your Recovery

I thought of you this morning,
And I said a little prayer,
That God in His great goodness,
Would keep you in His care . . .
I prayed that all the stormy clouds
Would disappear from view,
And only golden sunny skies
Would be ahead of you.

(© Paramount Line. All rights reserved.)

Valentines, Mother's Day cards, and wedding and anniversary cards are also using inspirationals with great success. The following inspirational was sold to Paramount a few years ago and still appears on their wedding and anniversary cards:

The Story of a Rose

God filled the earth with lovely blooms,
And scented them with rare perfumes,
And yet He knew one flower alone,
Was needed for true love to own.
And so He made the Rose with grace,

Perfected it in form and face,
He tended it until it grew
Into a beauty, rare and true.
And when its image was complete,
God made its fragrance warm and sweet,
Throughout all times its beauty grows,
And only LOVE outshines the Rose.

The inside text reads, "Happy Anniversary and warmest wishes to both of you for many future years of good health and happiness!"

Not all inspirationals are religious. Here is one of my nonreligious inspirationals which appeared first on a 50¢ Paramount Image card, and later was used on more expensive cards. It has been a best seller for the past five years and is still being used in Paramount's line:

Till There Was You

Till there was you each day that passed
Was like the day before.
Till there was you I didn't know
The joys life held in store.
But now the world is beautiful,
The earth, the sky above,
Embrace me with their gentleness . . .
For I have found true love.

Inside this same card, Paramount used another one of my nonreligious inspirationals entitled "Because of You":

Because of You

Because of you the bright stars shine,
My life is blessed, because you're mine.
Because of you my heart can sing
And even winter seems like spring.
Because of you I've dreams to share.
And laughter echoes everywhere . . .
Because of you, life holds much more,
For you make life worth living for.

With these two inspirationals, Paramount combined one of my four-line conventional verses, which said:

It's those we love who make the world
A happy place to be . . .
And loving you has brought a world
Of happiness to me.

Although all three of these card ideas were not purchased at the same time, the editors at Paramount knew how to combine them to create a best seller.

Most of the major card companies keep their eyes open for inspirationals which can be used in a variety of ways. Inspirationals that contain beautiful expressions about nature, God, faith, beauty, and other timeless truths will always be in great demand, as in the following:

Wishing You a Beautiful Day

God fills each day with beauty
From the oceans to the sky . . .
He paints the earth with miracles
To fill each wondering eye.
God fills each day with beauty
In the sea and on the land,
For all things bright and beautiful
Are touched by HIS sweet hand.

(© Paramount Line. All rights reserved.)

This particular inspirational could be used on a get well card, a birthday card, a seasonal card, a friendship card, or a thinking of you card, depending upon the particular needs of the company. By combining it with a simple "Hope your birthday is just beautiful," or "May your Easter be filled with all things bright and beautiful," the card company can use it over and over again to fit into their line at various times throughout the year.

All the major card companies have a large staff of greeting card writers, and the verses they purchase from freelancers *must* be exceptional ones. Card companies work on a strict budget, and quite often they have to pass up many well-written verses because they just can't afford to purchase them at the time they're sent in. Inspirationals that can be used in a variety of ways will have the best chance of selling, no matter how tight the card company's budget may be. Similarly, an inspirational poem that lends itself to many occasions will often be purchased immediately, while the more conventional verse will be sent back, even though the conventional verse may be exceptionally well written.

Friendship cards are becoming more popular today, too, and the following friendship verse is one that Paramount uses each year on its Image cards:

What Is Friendship?

Friendship's like the sun above,
That's always shining bright.
Friendship's like the golden smile,
That warms the coldest night . . .
Friendship is a priceless gift,
Of faithfulness and grace.
And nothing in the world can ever
Take true friendship's place!

This inspirational has appeared on friendship cards and also on birthday cards. Similar inspirationals of mine have been sold to manufacturers as ideas for plaques.

Getting ideas for writing inspirational cards is easier than you think. The Bible itself is the greatest single reference guide you can use. Psalms and the book of Revelation contain timeless truths which can inspire the writing of inspirational material. Ideals Publications is another source for getting ideas for inspirational verse, and Warner Press puts out inspirational booklets as well as cards, which can help you write good material of your own. Even song titles can often spark your imagination, as they did for me in my "Because of You" and "Till There Was You" verses. Reading published cards is another way to learn how to write good inspirationals. A good writer knows how to get ideas from published writers without copying!

For instance, one day I read a card that said, "Your friendship is a beautiful flower in my heart's garden." From this simple expression I composed a religious inspirational verse which was published by Warner Press:

The Garden of My Heart

Let me keep faith all else above,
And trust that can't depart.
When days seem long let me find a song,
In the garden of my heart.
Let me share the smiles of my many friends,
Even when my teardrops start,
Let me find the way to a brighter day
In the garden of my heart.
When my days seem spent and I've lost the light,
Of a dream that must depart,
Let me find the glow of the God I know
In the garden of my heart.

As you can see, my inspirational is nothing at all like the one I received my idea from, yet the original idea gave me a chance to develop an entirely different approach of my own.

If you want to write inspirational verses, you have to train yourself to look for that particular expression or timeless truth that you can use successfully to create your own inspirational material. You must also learn how to rhyme your verses so that they read smoothly and perfectly.

Inspirational writers are *not* free-verse writers! You can be both if you work hard at it, but you can't write good inspirational material if you don't know how to rhyme well.

You should also keep a notebook of all the beautiful expressions that appeal to you. Expressions like "Love is life's most precious gift," and "Faith can move mountains," may help you create a beautiful inspirational of your own.

Inspirational writing is not for the pessimist, nor is it for anyone who wants to sit down for two or three hours a week and jot off verses just to earn some extra money.

Believe me, there are easier ways to make a living than writing, but if you have the talent and the patience to develop your own style, you can make a name for yourself in this writing field.

When I began writing, I knew very little about the markets. My first attempts were typed on a single sheet of paper and mailed off to the Buzza Cardoza Card Company in California, addressed simply to "The Editor."

It was because of the kindness of Helen Farries that I received my first check, along with a list of do's and don't's for writing good verse. Here is the first inspirational I sold to Helen Farries for use on a wedding card:

The Beauty of Love

The most precious of gifts
Is known everywhere,
It's as ancient as time
And as free as the air.
It starts like a rose
That's been tended and grown
From a small simple seed
To a beauty well known.
If given much thought
It will grow through the years,
If left unattended
It soon disappears.
Its value is priceless,
And sent from above,
The greatest of all gifts
The Beauty of Love.

Later, I wrote hundreds of inspirational poems and conventional verse for Helen Farries, as well as for all the other major card companies. Paramount has been using my work for eight years, and many times they will put my name on the inspirationals, which is an added pleasure for any writer. *(Editor's note:* This practice varies from company to company and in different situations. Some companies prefer to use company-owned pen names.)

Inspirational verse is similar in style throughout most of the major card companies. Sometimes an editor may change a line or two of my verses to fit a particular need, but generally, most companies buy the same type of inspirational material. Verses of from eight to twelve lines are the best sellers, and if you can write a short conventional me-to-you sentiment to go with your longer inspirational verse, you will have a better chance of selling it.

The "What Is" type of card has also become a best seller throughout the card industry. Ideas range from "What Is a Grandma?" to "What Is Marriage . . . Life . . . A Home . . . A Mother?" and so on down the line. Following are two inspirational "What Is" cards which I have sold recently:

What Is Life?

Life is a flower,
A gift, bright as spring . . .
Life is warm laughter,
A heart that can sing . . .
Life is a loved one,
With soft, twinkling eyes . . .
Life is a rainbow,
Across cloudy skies . . .
Life is an ocean,
Where waves touch the shores . . .
Life is a sea bird,
That circles and soars . . .
Life is the sunlight,
That shines from above . . .
For life is the blessing,
God gives us with love . . .

and this one:

What Is a Grandmother?

The comfort of a soothing hand
When you are very small,
A patient voice, a listening ear,
As you are growing tall . . .
A guide whose wisdom is a source
Of knowledge that's worthwhile,
Who lovingly indulges you
So she can watch you smile . . .
A dear and special kind of friend
Whose love is always true,
For no one else in all the world
Means more to her than you . . .

These two inspirational poems were published by Paramount, but I have sold hundreds of similar ideas to Rust Craft, American Greetings, Norcross, and other companies who publish not only cards, but plaques as well.

Inspirational verses that express the beauty of nature or the wondrous gift of faith will always find a place in the greeting card market.

Millions of people search the card racks in their local stores every day, looking for an inspirational card that will uplift the hearts of the ones who will receive it. They're often willing to pay a little more for this type of card because they know that the one who receives it will most likely keep the card long after the occasion has been forgotten.

Most greeting card writers collect cards as feverishly as a stamp collector collects stamps. I myself have at least twenty scrapbooks of published cards which I have received over the years, along with ten scrapbooks of my own published cards. Many times just browsing through them gives me new ideas for writing more inspirational and conventional verses to send out. Granted, it takes time to organize your cards into books, but it also creates a world of new ideas for you to work with when you begin writing.

Writing is hard work, but it is also rewarding work. To be able to express love and warmth in the written word, and to know that millions of people are reading and enjoying your labors is the nicest reward a writer can obtain. I believe there is no greater satisfaction for a writer than to see his or her work bringing happiness and comfort to someone else. The inspirational card does this in a way that no other type of writing can do.

Although I write many different types of cards, I still feel the greatest thrill when I see one of my inspirationals in print. They're harder to write and they require a great deal of concentration, but to me, inspirationals are the nicest way I know of to say "I love you" to the entire world!

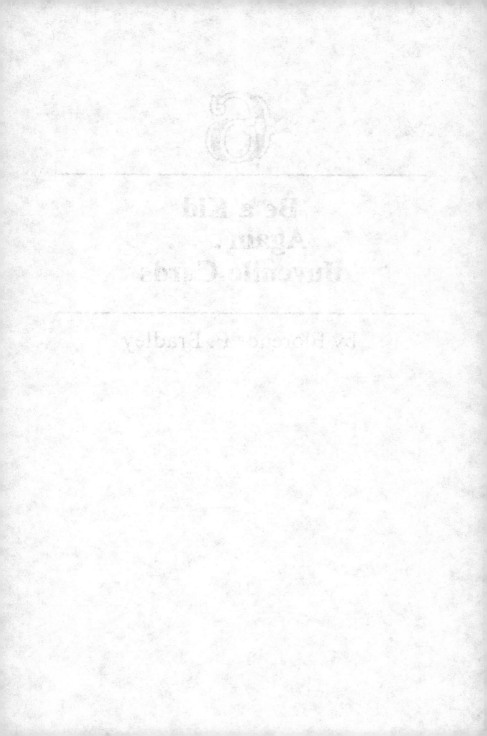

Be a Kid Again . . . Juvenile Cards

by Florence F. Bradley

Would you like to be a kid again for a few hours each day, drawing pictures, making rhymes, and playing games—and get paid for it? If you have patience, imagination, and understand children, you should try one of the most challenging, creative, and enjoyable forms of writing today—juvenile greeting cards.

It's a specialized field that involves hard work, research, and time. Sometimes one card can take half a day to do, from the time you think of it until you figure out all the angles to make it work, test it, and make the card itself. But the pay averages about $25 to $50 a piece, and that's not bad for half a day's work! Besides, they're such fun to do!

Good juvenile greeting card writers are hard to find, and if you can come up with original ideas that will hold a child's interest and be pleasing to adult buyers, you may soon find editors asking you to do special assignments—yes, you! And this chapter will tell you how to do it.

What *is* a juvenile card? It's a greeting card made especially to be sent to or sent by a child. There are basically two kinds: verse cards and activity cards.

The first type, *verse* cards, are just that—cards with a cute illustration on the front and a me-to-you message (just like in cards for grown-ups) on the inside. The message can be in rhymed verse or prose, and it can be either a direct message from the sender to the receiver, such as:

Hoping your birthday's
   as nice as can be—
The happiest birthday
   you ever did see!

Or it can be an indirect message that comes to the receiver by way of the animal or character pictured on the card, as in this example:

Here's Blabbit the Rabbit,
   who's hopping your way
To bring you this wish
   for a real HOPPY day!

I wouldn't advise you to start whipping off quick little four-line
verses like these to send off to editors, though. Most editors have all
of the simple, common ones like this that they need. What they
never seem to get enough of are the clever verses, the ones with new
thoughts or colorful words that make them pleasing to the ear, such
as this verse, published by Gibson Greeting Cards:

Hope your birthday's fun for you
And happy every minute
With lots of special birthday treats
And nice surprises in it!

The *minute/in it* rhyme helps to make this card appealing.
Bright, bouncy meter is what sets the following Christmas card for
a boy apart from all the rest:

Pa-rum-pa-pum-pum,
This drummer boy's drum
Is bringing a message your way—
Sure hope that your Christmas
Is merry and bright—
A really UNBEATABLE day!

Did you notice the wordplay, *unbeatable,* at the end of the verse?
Children love simple puns and wordplays, and if you're clever
enough you can use them as the basis of a nice juvenile card. Notice
how the following Gibson card was built around a series of wordplays involving bears and bees:

Hope your birthday finds you
      as happy as a bear
Who climbs a tree to find a beehive
      full of honey there . . .
And hope your year is swarmin'

with all it takes to see
That you're as happy every day
as you can BEAR to BEE!

Wordplay is not limited to puns, either. Playing with word sounds is another possibility, as the following card demonstrates:

[*outside*]   [*art: friendly-looking tiger*]
Birthday Grrreetings!

[*inside*]   Grrracious me!
How fast you're
Grrrowing Up!
HAPPY BIRTHDAY

Keep in mind, as you play with clever rhyme, meters, sounds, and such, that it is not enough to have a card that is pleasing to the ear. First and foremost, the card must carry a message—a wish, a compliment, or a special thought that is appropriate for the occasion. Most general cards feature wishes or compliments. They may be geared to very young children, like this complimentary birthday card:

You're cute as a button
   from head to toe,
And you keep getting cuter
   the bigger you grow!
HAPPY BIRTHDAY

Or they can be written for older children, like this valentine, also complimentary:

RT-10 from outer space—
(for short they call him "Artie")
Has come with all his friends
To have a Valentine's Day party . . .
Sure hope that you can join them
'cause they all agree it's true—
There's no one in the galaxy
More likable than you!

In all cases when writing general juvenile cards, keep your verses general so they can be sent to any girl or boy. Also keep in mind that not all cards for children are sent by adults. Many are purchased for one child to give to another.

Cards for young *family members* are usually complimentary and often add a few words of love. They can be clever, like the following birthday card for a niece. But, like this card, they should also be very warm:

[*outside*]   *To a Special Niece with Love*

[*inside*]   Know what kind of girl you are?
                It's really plain to see . . .
                Begin by spelling "NIECE,"
                Then just remove the middle "E"!
                          You're Nice!
                Hope your birthday's nice, too!

A large percentage of juvenile greeting card sales comes from the second type of card, the *activity* card. There are several kinds of activity cards—games, quizzes, puzzles, and things to make or do. Such cards are especially prized by children, which gives the card added value. This makes activity cards especially appropriate for higher-priced juvenile cards, and you'll notice that most juvenile cards in the higher price ranges have some sort of activity or other novelty such as a pop-up included. For this reason, editors are usually on the lookout for new activity card ideas, and they're often willing to pay a premium for an idea that can be published inexpensively, and developed into a bestselling juvenile card. Here are some examples of activity cards that I have sold to editors over the years.

A *game* card that I designed originated one winter when I saw a field mouse running across the snow. I wondered if a cat would get him before he found a warm place to hide. "That's an idea for a game card," I thought. So I dashed to my desk, and made a list of all the things I could think of that could delay a little mouse trying to get in out of the snow. Here are some that I came up with:

He could fall into a snowbank
He could get caught in a mousetrap
A cat could get him
He could stop to eat a piece of cheese

Next, I wondered, "How could this be made into a greeting card?" Putting two little mice in the bottom lefthand corner of the card, I made spaces back and forth, across the card (with tiny mouse tracks in them, just for effect) that led to a nice warm house in the top righthand corner. I played around with this for a while, and decided the game should be played by two children, each trying to get their mouse into the house first, by picking up little cards telling them how many spaces to move. They would try to avoid getting caught by each of the obstacles mentioned above, plus many others I came up with. After *my* children tried the game and gave it their seal of approval, I put a verse on the front:

Birthdays are a fun day,
And so I've sent to you
A *wish* for a fun day,
And a game that's fun to *do.*

Then I sent it to an editor. I hope the little mouse in the field found a warm place to live. He made me $25!

Quizzes and puzzles make good get well cards. A bedridden youngster welcomes a challenge, to break the monotony. I got just such an idea from a pet shop that's not too far from our house. One day I wandered inside to see a pair of white huskies from Alaska, or wherever huskies come from. I was impressed with the varieties of dogs they had there. There seemed to be one from nearly every country. Suddenly I had an idea for a quiz card.

At home, I got out my *Golden Book Dictionaries,* looked up dogs, and found half a page of them! Sure enough, they came from all different countries. When I made the card, I drew all types of dogs all around it, with a list of countries in the middle. The child was to draw a line from the dog to its nationality (English Bull, Irish Setter, etc.). The verse topped off the idea:

The day goes slow when you're in bed!
You'd rather be outside, instead.
So all these dogs have come to play
And help you pass the time away.

And my card was finished. A most profitable trip to the pet store!

Notice that the verse on an activity card tends to tie in with the activity, giving the child some idea of what is coming.

The next type of activity card has something to make or do. Here's how one of mine came about:

My daughter had been given a shot for virus, and she got even with the doctor by drawing a very unflattering picture of him, with a long hypodermic needle in his hand. I turned the idea over in my mind while I did the dishes. Most children like to draw, and they certainly have time to when they're sick in bed.

I made my daughter a *dummy* card, just to try out my idea. On the front, I printed:

You're sick?
Well don't just lie there feeling sad!
Being sick isn't all that bad!
So get a pencil and begin
And I'll bet your pictures bring a grin!

Inside I wrote:

This is my doctor (He's making me well)

And I left a space for her to draw her doctor. Next it said:

This is my mommy (She treats me swell!)
This is my medicine (It don't taste the best)
And this one is me (Getting lots of rest)

My daughter was delighted, and asked me to make another one. I did—but this time I sent it off to an editor. And she bought it.

I guess the most important thing in writing juvenile activity cards is getting good ideas. Where do I get ideas for my cards? Just about everywhere. Children's books and magazines are a good place to

start. You often can find an idea in a book or magazine, change it
around, and come up with something new and appealing.

Television and movies are another good source of ideas . . .
children's games can often be adapted to greeting cards. Many of
my children's cards come from games I played in my childhood,
sometimes putting a new twist on an old idea.

Perhaps most of all, I *really* pay attention to the everyday situations around me, and adapt them for juvenile cards.

Let's take a look at some of the successful ideas I've derived from
the above sources, and sold to various greeting card companies.

First on the list is children's books and magazines. A good illustrated children's dictionary or encyclopedia is worth its weight in
gold. Its illustrations are wonderful. If I'm not sure how many toes
to put on the animal I'm drawing, or which way the stripes go on a
zebra, I can always find out by looking it up. When I'm stuck for
ideas, leafing through a volume or two usually gives me several.

Children's magazines are an excellent place to look for salable
ideas. *Humpty Dumpty* has lots of mechanical things to do, and I've
gotten many ideas from it. *Jack and Jill* once gave me an idea that
resulted in a $75 sale for three cards, all based on the same idea.
Here's how it happened.

My children's copy of *Jack and Jill* was lying open on the floor.
When I picked it up, I noticed a little Halloween story that had
blanks in it, every other sentence or so. I remembered playing that
as a child, and my money brain decided to try it for a greeting card.
At the time Barker Greeting Cards (now a division of Rust Craft)
was doing valentines, so I wrote the following little story:

> Cupid had a problem. His two favorite friends, John, who just
> loves _____ , and Joan, who is very much like_____ ,
> didn't have Valentines to love! Everyone needs _____to be
> happy on Valentine's Day! Cupid set out to solve the problem.
> He sent_____ the color of_____to Joan, and he signed it
> from _____ . Then he shot_____from his bow at John.
> Next Cupid mixed a love potion of_____and_____ .
> And he stirred it with_____. Then he put some
> in_____ for Joan, and the rest into_____ for John. And it

worked! Before you could say_____, Joan and John fell in love. They got married on St. Valentine's Day, and they sent Cupid_____to say "Thank you."

I had little words and phrases such as *pet, frog, a spoon, a cupcake, a flower, a car, a tree, a bathtub, the front porch, sugar, money, a cardboard box, a secret,* and *a blue bottle,* which were to be cut out and inserted in the blanks as the story was read. Changing the sequence of the words and phrases makes the story come out differently every time you read it. Try it.

The editor at Barker liked it well enough to ask me to make two more cards like it—one with a Christmas story, and one with an Easter story.

Highlights for Children, Cricket, Ranger Rick, and *National Geographic World* are also good sources of ideas for children, as are magazines that children get in school, such as the *Scholastic* magazines and the *Weekly Reader* series.

Let's take a look at getting ideas from movies and television. At a time when secret agents were popular, I wanted to find an idea for older boys (aged 9-12). I know this age group is interested in challenging things like sports or mysteries to solve, and I finally hit on a decoding wheel that could be used to decode a Valentine message inside the card, and also to send secret messages to friends. The verse on the front tied it in with the hero of the day:

We're both secret agents,
And the message I've sent
Is in secret code, so—
To find what I meant,
You'll have to de-code it,
—Look inside for the way.
And see what I'm wishing
For Valentine's Day!

By the time this one sold, I'd had to make the decoding wheel for my sons and half of their friends. It was a very big hit in our neighborhood.

The Philadelphia 76'ers basketball team has a lot of fans at our house, and for a while there, it seemed like every time I turned around, there was another basketball game on television. Finally I gave in, and watched one. Gee, it looked like fun, throwing that ball through the hoop!

Always looking for greeting card ideas, I tried to figure out how to put the game on a card, and devised a cardboard setup that had two basketball hoops inside, to be cut out and bent to stand up. It had circles to be cut out to pitch pennies or buttons through.

My only problem was that the game took up the entire inside of the card, leaving no room for instructions. So I had to be sure that the verse on the front explained what the card was about. I came up with this one that filled the bill:

> You're getting to be such a big boy and all,
> I've sent this game of basketball.
> With a little cutting, a few small bends,
> And you're ready to play it with your friends.

Now I'm a 76'ers fan, too!

Next we come to *games* that can be adapted for greeting cards. The first game that pops into my tired brain is *bingo*. I sold that one not only once, but twice!—thanks to my four-year-old. She wanted to play bingo with the older children, and they told her, "You can't play, you don't know your numbers!"

Trying to comfort her, I said, "I'll make you a bingo game you can play!" And I did. The game had colors on the cards instead of numbers. A spinner was provided, and each time a child spun a color, he was allowed to cover one square of that color on his card. It worked very well and, with the following verse, brought me a tidy sum as a juvenile greeting card:

> I hope you have fun on your birthday,
> And to help make sure you do,
> I picked this special birthday card
> With a game inside for you.

Looking through my "sold" file a few months later (another

place to get ideas), I came across the color bingo game. I was doing juvenile Christmas cards, and I decided to try the bingo idea again, this time using pictures of toys instead of numbers. It was fun, tied with the season, and could be played by all children—for what child doesn't know toys? The verse on that one read:

Hi there! Merry Christmas!

No need to wait till Christmas,
Start having fun right now.
Play Santa's brand-new Bingo game,
Inside tells you how . . .

This was one of the cards that took nearly half a day to do, drawing all those little toys on the bingo cards. When I started doing juvenile greeting cards—several years ago—I couldn't draw worth a darn. But I soon found that the cards I took the time to illustrate brought me the most money, so I kept trying, and it gets easier as I go along. If you can't draw very well either, don't be discouraged—just do the best you can; you can get by with just enough of an illustration to help put your idea across to the editor. And you'll find it becomes easier with practice. Besides, those fatter checks make it well worth the time!

A good way to get started doing juvenile cards is to delve into your own childhood. You've probably seen paper dolls and punch-out cowboys on children's cards. They're very good sellers. Why? Because adults buy the cards that are sent to children, and most adults played paper dolls or cowboys when they were children. They remember nostalgically the old and familiar games they played, so they buy the cards that have them. Appeal to the adult, and your card will be a good seller. For that reason, many of my children's cards were based on things I enjoyed as a child, and that my children enjoy doing now.

For instance, one evening while sitting on my front steps watching my daughters play hopscotch, I got the bright idea that that too could be turned into a juvenile activity card. The problem was to get hopscotch, which took up my whole sidewalk, onto a little card about ten or eleven inches wide. I used the regular hopscotch pattern in miniature and had my children try to toss pennies into each square, without landing on the lines. The first one to get all the way to the end won the game. They liked it. I called it Penny Hopscotch, added a verse—

Get a penny for you
and one for a pal,
And play penny hopscotch,
inside tells you how!

—and promptly turned the idea into a check from Gibson Greetings. (Incidentally, I did the same thing with shuffleboard, using pencils and buttons and a miniature shuffleboard.)

So, what games did *you* enjoy as a child? Maybe they're worth money in the juvenile activity card market!

Juvenile cards are done in about three age groups: the 3-6, 6-9, and 9-12 age levels. So when I'm working on juveniles, I try to do some the older child will enjoy, and some for the younger child. For instance, a quiz I had once done with the younger children in mind popped into my head when one of my children printed her name. The letters were all there, but in the wrong order. I had been looking for ideas for Christmas activity cards and used the idea of scrambled names. The verse explains the card:

A Christmas Problem

Santa went shopping and bought four pair
Of pretty collars for his reindeer to wear.
He painted them quick, before the reindeer could see,
But he got the names scrambled as they can be.

Inside were the collars waiting for the child to unscramble the names on them. As usual, I put the correct answers inside the card, in case the child got stuck.

As I said before, one of the best ways I've found of getting ideas for juvenile greeting cards is by observing what goes on around me every day and adapting these things to cards. (Of course it helps to have six children to get ideas from!)

I think one of the best ideas I ever came up with was one that saved me a lot of backbreaking work. We were making a snowman in our front yard, and as he got bigger and bigger, Mommy was the first to get tired. As I staggered into the house for a cup of hot chocolate, I thought, "There must be an easier way to make a snowman!"

Leave it to tired old me to come up with one, and naturally, once I did, it found its way onto a greeting card! It turned out to be a game that the whole family could enjoy. On the front of the card all I had to put was a big picture of a snowman, complete with a top hat, and the words:

Mr. Snowman and I bring you Christmas fun.

Inside was a spinner, with a head, buttons, top hat—the works—on it. The object: to be first to spin a complete snowman like the one on the front of the card.

Now when the kids say, "Mom, let's make a snowman," I dig out the greeting card snowman game, and that's that, as far as I'm concerned!

There is a special way to come up with ideas for seasonal cards for the juvenile greeting card market. I make a list of all the things that have to be done—say, for Christmas—and a list of all the things I can think of in connection with the season, such as holly, tree, candles. And I reread these lists until something jells in my mind and gives me an idea for a card. For instance, I got $50 for an original Christmas game that I came up with using this method: The card had two Christmas trees inside, and a spinner. On the spinner was tinsel, balls, an angel, candy canes, etc. Several of each of these things were also pictured on little markers to be cut out. Whenever a child spun something he needed to trim his tree, he took a marker with that item on it and placed it on his tree. First one to trim his tree won. Original? Yes. Fun for a child? Yes. Time-consuming to make? Yes. But profitable for me! . . . and, I hope, for the greeting card company, too!

This same company took an original game I did that had children drawing cards to complete their Christmas shopping lists.

Both of these ideas came from my "list of things to do." Everyone has a gift list to complete. Just about everyone trims a tree for Christmas. Making a list of these things could easily give you an idea for still another type of Christmas game. Try it! (You might also get the idea for a "trimming the Christmas tree game" while you're trimming your tree in December, but when July rolls around and you're doing Christmas cards, you forget that stuff. Hence the lists!)

An important thing to remember about original game cards is that you are the only one who knows how the game is to be played. Write down the rules. Study them. Then rewrite them, giving clear, simple directions that a child can understand. Make sure everything the child needs to know to play the game is there.

Then, if possible, give the game to a child or two, preferably about the age the card is intended for. Let them read the directions and play the game. Alone.

You may be surprised. Your rules may be far from clear. Or you may need more markers or little cards than you thought. Some ideas simply will not work out. And some games just are not fun at all. Now is your chance to fix them up, or scrap them, before an editor sees them.

As an example, let's look at the directions I gave for the Christmas tree game I just mentioned:

Trim the Christmas Tree (for two players)

You each take turns spinning to get the decorations you need to trim your Christmas tree. The first player who trims his tree wins. To win, you must get:

    4 balls (1 each of green, yellow, red, and blue)
    2 tinsels
    2 candy canes
    1 angel treetop

Each time you spin, put the decoration the spinner points to on your tree. (There are extra decorations in case you lose some.) If you spin a blank or a decoration you already have, you lose that turn and the other player spins.

Let me inject a bit of my own philosophy here. There are two rules you should always remember about doing games for juvenile greeting cards. Always make sure your work is original, and always, *always* test it before you send it out. I have talked to nearly every editor I've sold to. They *try* the games. They *do* the quizzes and puzzles. You'd be surprised how many of my games wouldn't have sold if I hadn't found out beforehand that they weren't quite workable at first. If you don't have children around, play the game yourself. Take the place of each player. A good idea is to put blanks in for lost turns to make a game last longer, and for more suspense. Put the answers to quizzes and puzzles inside the cards—the editor shouldn't have to figure them out—and make sure you didn't forget anything.

It's hard work. You can't afford to spend half a day on an idea that isn't good. Carbon copies of other cards on the market won't sell.

Besides, there is no end of places to get ideas. Look at the world as a child does. There are dozens of ideas on the toy counters of the typical variety or discount store, waiting to be adapted to juvenile cards. Watch the children around you. I sold a "penny saver" card when I saw my son working on his coin collection. I did a puzzle in the shape of a heart for Valentine's Day. I sold a card for children in bed to make shadow pictures on the wall. And watching children look for the golden egg in an Easter egg hunt resulted in a game that sold to Hallmark.

If you have a good, original game, puzzle, or quiz but are afraid the verse on it isn't good enough, send the idea in anyway. A good verse won't sell a poor idea, but if your activity is good and your verse doesn't measure up, you may get a check for the idea but find the company has returned your verse, preferring to do its own.

Although this chapter has dealt, up to now, strictly with cards designed to be sent to children, there is also a large number of cards produced and purchased each year to be sent *by* children to adults. These are generally limited to family captions such as Mom, Dad, Grandma, Grandpa, Aunt, and Uncle. Most are verse cards, though occasionally there is a card that is designed for the child to color or add some other personal touch to.

As in all juvenile cards, a certain amount of cleverness, a pleasant rhyme or wordplay, may be used to enhance the card. Here is a Gibson "Aunt" Valentine with a touch of humor:

> [*outside*]   [*art: cute bear talking on telephone*]
> Hello, Aunt!
> Happy Valentine's Day!
>
> [*inside*]   Sent this card to say, "Hello"
> And here's the reason why—
> 'Cause you're an Aunt who's loved a lot . . .
> That's all for now—Goodbye!

Of course there's more than just a humorous ending to this card. It contains a wish and a message of love. Most child-to-adult cards have either a wish or a compliment, and almost all say in one way or another "I love you!"

When writing juvenile cards, as when writing any type of card, it's important to know what your editors are looking for. One editor might be interested in all types of ideas, while another might need only activity cards. Sometimes an editor might have a specific need such as Christmas cards for children to send to "Mommy." By going to the trouble to find out what an editor needs, you can save both yourself and the editor a lot of time, and you can use that time to concentrate on ideas that are more likely to sell.

Once you have a group of terrific ideas together, send them out. Don't worry too much about rejections—you'll get them. Everybody does. Just keep sending your ideas out. If they're really good and really original, some are going to sell along the way. After your cards have made the rounds, try to improve on the ones that haven't sold, and send them out again, a year later. If they still don't sell and you think they have merit, cut off the verses and send just the game or idea part to children's magazines or Sunday-school papers that buy fillers. This may not bring as much as cards, but it'll help pay back the postage money!

If, as happens, you have a game that is really good but too

expensive for a company to put on a greeting card, send it to a game manufacturer. Maybe you'll sell it there.

You can see there are lots of ways to have fun and make money in the juvenile activity card or verse market. It's well worth the effort, for the pay is pretty good. Besides, it's certainly a great feeling when you get one of *your* finished cards in the mail from a thoughtful editor. Or find one unexpectedly on a counter in your own neighborhood drugstore. And the first time you send one of *your* cards to your own favorite youngster, you won't trade this business for any other in the world.

Light and Bright . . . Informals

by Dick Lorenz

G enerally speaking, a greeting card is an illustrated wish or sentiment. A successful greeting card is one in which the mood generated by the art is carried through by (and perhaps expanded upon by) the copy. In no area is this more apparent than in the type of cards known in the business as *cutes* or *informals*.

An eight-line conventional verse might well be used with art consisting of a bouquet of flowers, or soft-focus photography. Many studio cards could successfully employ the same neuter character wearing a funny hat and holding its index finger aloft. The *informal* idea, however, relies heavily upon the situation depicted on the cover of the card tying in with the message.

You can "write" an eight-line verse for a conventional card. You can "write" a studio card. But you cannot "write" an informal; you must *conceptualize* an informal. (Or, at the very least, your end product must appear as though the art and idea sprang into being as one.) In fact, informals are sometimes referred to as *situation* cards.

Notice how an art suggestion helps to get the idea across:

[*Suggested art: Cute female putting icing on cake*]

[*page 1*]   A little confection . . .

[*page 3*]   with a lot of affection!
                    HAPPY BIRTHDAY

[*Suggested art: Cute female listening to old-fashioned record player*]

[*page 1*]   Just for the record . . .

[*page 3*]   you're one year nicer!
                    HAPPY BIRTHDAY

While the visual aspect of an informal card cannot be stressed too strongly, there are other properties to be considered.

Informals are, as the word implies, *casual, comfortable, relaxed,* and *uncomplicated.* The copy should be *light and bright, concise and nice.* Here's a rare informal that's eight lines long:

[*Art: Cute animals dancing in a circle*]

[*page 1*]   Happy Birthday!

[*page 3*]   Hope your birthday's a mirth day,
                    A heaven-on-earth day,
                    A go-and-enjoy-it-
                    For-all-that-it's-worth day . . .
                    And then have a glad year,
                    A never-be-sad year,
                    A perfectly wonderful,
                    Best-one-you've-had year!

Most informals are more direct and to the point. Here's one that's more in keeping with the normal length:

[*Art: Cute puppy with floppy ears*]

[*page 1*]   Hope this is your happiest birthday . . .

[*page 3*]   in all your "born days"!

Informals can be whimsical:

[*Art: Little mermaid diving into water*]

[*page 1*]   It's your day . . .

[*page 3*]   Make a big splash

They can be sentimental:

[*Art: Rear view of couple sitting on fence in bucolic setting*] [*page 1*]   It's a beautiful world . . .

[*page 3*]   when it's shared by two!
                   HAPPY ANNIVERSARY

They can have a touch of religion:

[*Art: Cute female in Early American clothes, working on needle-point that says "BLESS YOU"*]

[*page 3*]   . . . and make you well.

They can be somewhat sophisticated:

[*Art: Coy, stylized, up-to-date woman*]

[*No copy on page 1*]

[*page 3*]   I just love older men!

Informals can be in prose, as in the previous examples, or in rhyme, with couplets as a popular vehicle:

[*Art: Cute character cutting birthday cake*]

[*page 1*]   Wishing you a birthday slice . . .

[*page 3*]   of everything that's extra nice!
                   HAPPY BIRTHDAY

[*Art: Cute character picking wildflowers*]

[*page 1*]   Hopin' your birthday is nicer 'n flowers . . .

[*page 3*]   and brings you a bunch
                   of the happiest hours!
                   HAPPY BIRTHDAY

To better understand informals it might be helpful to know why and how they came into being. In 1962 several members of the creative staff of Norcross presented a new grouping of cards (the original informals) to the late Arthur Norcross as a possible addition to the Norcross Humor Line. The thinking behind those cards was to offer the public something lighter than the conventional line, smarter than the humor line, and not as harsh as the studio line.

Norcross was very enthusiastic about the concept, but felt that rather than simply incorporate the cards into the humor line, they should be produced and marketed as a separate entity. Their success was immediate, and informals (by whatever name each company uses for them) remain an important part of the greeting card market.

While informals have their own distinct traits, always keep this very important point in mind when attempting to create them: *Like any other type of greeting card, informals must express a me-to-you message, a message that is relevant enough and meaningful enough for a customer to be willing to spend his or her hard-earned cash on.* It could be a wish, a compliment, or a special thought. Editors are looking mostly for ideas for traditional greeting-card-sending situations—birthdays, get wells, and such. If you have an idea that you believe in, one that you think would appeal to thousands of potential card buyers, don't worry too much about whether or not it falls into an established category. Good editors are always on the lookout for good, original ideas, no matter what the category.

Writing
for the
Humorous Market

by Larry Sandman

One of the most curious things to me, as an editor of both studio and humorous lines, is how *many* freelance writers are writing studio, and how *few* are writing humorous cards. I could count on two hands the number of writers who submit humorous card ideas to me with any regularity. Studios? I can't keep up with them all!

But when I call it a "curious thing," I'm not implying that I can't see any reason for it. Actually, the reason can be summed up in one short line—humorous cards are harder to write. It's true! Generally speaking a humorous card takes more time and more thought than a studio card, and in freelancing, as in any other form of business, time means money.

Why, then, am I surprised that there are perhaps twenty studio writers for every humorous writer submitting greeting card ideas today? Because of that very fact, that I am receiving studio submissions at twenty times the rate of humorous ideas. This means the competition in the studio market is twenty times as stiff as the competition in the humorous market (give or take a few times).

If these figures make you want to stop and think for a minute about the humorous market, and I hope they do, then read on. Perhaps you'll find that knowing a little more about humorous cards, what they are, and how they're written, will persuade you to take a crack at this underexploited market. Hey, there's nothing wrong with writing studio cards. I do it myself! All I'm saying is, why not branch out and write humorous, too?

I've felt for some time that a lot of people have overlooked the humorous market simply because they don't really know the line is there. Many writers, I believe, think that humorous is just another name for studio. Not true. Humorous cards are a distinct line of greetings that express a sentiment in a funny, clever, or cute way. The name "humorous" is in itself deceiving. It suggests that all the cards are funny, which isn't true. Many humorous cards are more "sweet" than funny, as this Valentine for Mother shows:

[*outside*]   *For a Wonderful Mother*
      on Valentine's Day
     One flowery phrase that says it all . . .

[*inside*]   [*written in flowers*]
      LOVE YOU A BUNCH!
     HAPPY VALENTINE'S DAY!

Other humorous cards tend more toward the clever. They aim to make you smile, not laugh:

[*outside*]   [*computer feeding out data*]
     All the REASONS, Dad,
      may not be computable . . .

[*inside*]   But you're "one-in-a-million"—
      that's indisputable!
     HAPPY FATHER'S DAY

Then there are the humorous cards that are actually intended to be funny. They have sentiments that could just as easily appear in the studio line. Here's an example:

[*outside*]   It's Father's Day
     and you deserve a 21-gun salute . . .

[*inside*]   . . . or at least a couple of "shots"!
     HAPPY FATHER'S DAY!

The difference between this and a studio card is in the way it's illustrated. In fact, what distinguishes humorous cards from *all* the other lines is the way they're illustrated. Humorous cards are actually written with a particular illustration or situation in mind. It's for this reason that many people in the business refer to them as *illustrated* cards.

When you write a humorous card, it is best to start out thinking visually. Think of how the idea could be illustrated. While it takes some extra thought to visualize a card, humorous cards do allow the writer a high degree of flexibility. Unlike studios and unlike most informals, humorous cards do not have a standard size or shape. They can be tall or squarish, they can fold out or down, they can have pop-ups or die-cut holes, special folds and finishes, they can be drawings or photographs, or even drawings superimposed over photographs—the possibilities are many.

The sentiments, too, can be done in many ways. They can be short prose, not unlike studio sentiments:

[*outside*]   [*photo of two pigs*]
                 Let's get together on your birthday . . .

[*inside*]   . . . and have a snort or two!

They can be silly couplets:

[*outside*]   [*baboon pounding on drum*]
                 FOR SOMEONE WHO'S SICK
                     A little BABOOM

[*inside*]   . . . to drive the gloom from the room!
                     GET WELL SOON!

They can be nice, pleasant four-line verses:

[*outside*]   [*cute animal in bed; sun hiding behind clouds*]
                 The sun can't shine
                     as bright as it should . . .

[*inside*]   [*animal out of bed; sun shining*]
                 Till you're up and about again . . .
                     feeling good!

They can be cheery eight-line verses:

[*outside*]   [*each attribute illustrated separately, such as
                 "Mom" baking cookies for "thoughtful," help-
                 ing make bed for "a help," etc.*]

Is There a Perfect Mom?
A Mom who's always thoughtful?
Who's a help in many ways?

[inside]   Who's always understanding?
Who can brighten gloomy days?
Who's proud of all your triumphs?
Who's consoling when you goof?
There really *is* that kind of Mom . . .
And *you're* the *loving proof!*

Or they can be something totally unique, not quite like anything
you'll find in any other line:

[outside]   [*designed to look like an insurance policy*]
GOOD HEALTH POLICY
of the
CONVALESCENT BENEFIT
ASSOCIATION
Issued by the Good Health Underwriters

[inside]   The Convalescent Benefit Association
Underwriters for GOOD HEALTH Inc.
under the law of the state of health and happiness
THIS POLICY
entitles the holder

M _____

to a speedy recovery
an end to all aches and pains,
and years of
HEALTH, HAPPINESS, AND CONTENT-
MENT

Signed on the _____

day of _____ 19 _____

by _____
General Agent for Good Health

   Notice that in each of these examples the sentiment is very closely tied to the design. That isn't usually the case in studios, where the same neuter character could be used to illustrate several different sentiments.

   Humorous cards can be divided into several established formats, based on their sentiment types and lengths, and their design characteristics. We've already seen examples of short, prose, studiolike cards, as well as two-, four-, and eight-line illustrated verses.

   One of the oldest, and still one of the most popular, formats is the long *illustrated verse*, in which each individual phrase is separately illustrated. Here's a typical example of such illustrated verse:

[*outside*]   *A Valentine for My Sweetheart*
         More than BEES love to BUZZ . . .
         More than BEARS love to SLEEP . . .

[*inside*]   More than FISH love to SWIM . . .
         More than FROGS love to LEAP . . .
         More than BIRDS love to SING . . .
         More than COWS love to MOO . . .
         More than ANYTHING, Sweetheart,
         I love LOVING YOU!
         HAPPY VALENTINE'S DAY!

   Illustrated verses can be light and whimsical, like the one above, or more realistic, bordering on seriously sentimental, like the following verse:

[*outside*]   *What Is a Mother?*
         She's a banker and a chauffeur
            and a full-time referee

[*inside*]   She's a sanitation expert
      and a practicing M.D.
    She's a teacher and a counselor
      with very good advice
    She's a great short-order cook
      and she's a friend who's really nice
    So what, then, is a Mother?
      Seems the answer's pretty clear—
    She's a lot of special people
      and they're all especially dear!
    HAPPY MOTHER'S DAY

All illustrated verses have several things in common. They lend themselves well to illustration, they all progress to a logical conclusion, and they all carry legitimate me-to-you messages. They're dressed up to be light and fun, but their underlying messages are uniformly warm and pleasant.

Another type of humorous format is the *parody*. Many things can be the basis for a humorous parody card: newspapers, magazines, wanted posters, book covers—even other cards make likely targets for humorous parodies.

Both Gibson and Hallmark have done humorous parodies of a TV-guide type of magazine. Gibson did it for an Illness, Hospital card; Hallmark, on a Birthday card. Both used the general format of a TV-guide magazine, but changed the programs to funny titles, appropriate for the card. The Gibson parody, for example, featured such programs as "Scalpel Street"—where today's episode has brain surgery being performed on Big Birdie—"Hollywood Scars," "What's My Spine," and "Name That Prune."

American Greetings has had a lot of success with their parodies of newspapers, one the Birthday Edition of *The High Old Times,* and another, *The Get Well News.* Both are full of funny, farfetched articles on their respective subjects.

Parodies like this take a good deal of time and work, and so they rarely come from freelancers. If well done, however, such works would command a premium price in some companies. There are countless things that could lend themselves to parodies, things from diplomas to stock certificates to confession magazines.

Related to parodies, though not quite the same, are *signs, badges, and certificates.* I've lumped these all into one format, though each is a distinct idea in itself. Many of the major companies produce humorous cards with signs, badges, certificates, or some other type of bonus either on or in the card. Made out of paper, and perforated around the edges so that it can be removed, such a prize adds a lot of value to a card in the eyes of card customers.

We've already seen the "Good Health Policy" for a get well card. Another certificate-type card is this "Mother of the Year" award:

[*outside*]   *For a Special Mother*
               A Mother's Day Award
               For always being thoughtful,
                   patient, loving, sweet and dear . . .

[*inside*]   You've hereby earned the title
               of the Mother of the Year!

The inside of the card bears a certificate that applauds all of Mother's attributes, and it is meant to be signed and dated by the sender. Similar cards include one with a "Mom Appreciation" coupon inside, which promises that the sender will relieve "Mom" of all domestic chores for the day, and another contains a special "credit card" for someone who deserves "special credit for always being thoughtful, generous, loving, and caring."

Another humorous format is the *photo tie-in* card. This is a humorous card which features a photograph—often an animated object, or a cartoon character dropped into a photographic setting. Close-up photos of fruits and vegetables, consumer products, hardware, household goods, and the like are given life through drop-in art. The sentiment is made to tie in somehow with the subject of the photograph, for example:

[*outside*]   [*photo: close-up of pumpkin—pumpkin has
               dropped-in cartoon eyes and smile*]
               You're not getting older . . .

[*inside*]   You're just getting ripe!
                    HAPPY BIRTHDAY!

Another photo tie-in card features two chimps on the outside with
banana peels on their heads:

[*outside*]   Birthdays have a certain *appeal,* it's true . . .

[*inside*]   But I'm glad they don't come in *bunches,*
                    aren't you?

                    HAPPY BIRTHDAY!

Photo tie-in messages can be short or long, rhymed verse or
prose, using a single photograph or a series of shots. They must
connect in some clever, cute, or funny way with the photograph,
and they must, of course, carry an appropriate me-to-you message.

Another popular format is the humorous *mechanical* card. These
were quite popular several years ago, but they declined somewhat
when their production costs started becoming prohibitive. Recent
increases in the numbers of high-priced humorous cards are making many mechanicals feasible again. Mechanical cards are particularly appealing to customers because there is some sort of action
when the card is opened.

One common type of mechanical card is the pop-up. A *pop-up*
card is, just as the name suggests, a card in which part of the inside
design pops up as the card is opened. Just as in photo tie-in cards,
where the sentiment must be connected in some way to the photo,
so the sentiment in a pop-up card should tie in with the mechanical
action. Here are a couple of examples of how it is done:

[*outside*]   [*tired-looking mare*]
                    THE OLD GRAY MARE
                        Ain't what she used to be . . .

[*inside*]   [*mare kicking, hind legs pop up*]
                    But there's plenty of KICK
                        in the OLD TALE yet!
                    HAPPY BIRTHDAY!

[*outside*]   [*volcano with sad face*]
                     Not feeling in PEAK condition?

[*inside*]   [*pop-up of volcano erupting*]
                     Hope you're soon on the ACTIVE list again!

Cards can also be designed to pop down or pop out. Here's a good example of a card with a pop-down:

[*outside*]   YOU'RE 29 TODAY?

[*inside*]   [*pop-down: crocodile's mouth opening*]
                     What a CROC!
                     HAPPY BIRTHDAY!

Another type of mechanical is what is called a *slider*. This is a card that is folded and die-cut in such a way that part of the inside slides when the card is opened. One particularly effective slider is the following card which features a slot machine. When the card is opened, three birthday cakes slide into view in the three windows of the machine:

[*outside*]   Slotted for a birthday?

[*inside*]   Pullin' for a happy one for you!

Special *die-cuts* provide yet another humorous format. Die-cutting holes in special places on cards can open up possibilities for both design and editorial. Here's an old best seller from Gibson that benefits from a particularly clever use of a die-cut:

[*outside*]   *A Birthday "Peephole"*
                     For men only!
                     Just peek inside and you'll see
                     sumpin' cute!
                     [*die-cut hole in fence; see through to what appears to be legs of a slender young woman*]

[*inside*]   Here she is, Mister!
                             Ain't she a Beaut!
                             HAPPY BIRTHDAY,
                             YOU OL' REPROBATE!
                             [*inside design: cow; legs that appeared to be-
                             long to woman belong to the cow*]

There are no doubt other humorous formats that have not been covered in this chapter. Perhaps, as you let your imagination go, working with folds, cuts, design concepts, and such, you will come up with a new format of your own. The humorous line is unusual in that it houses side by side a good deal of old, traditional, proven material, and also many recent innovations.

There are opportunities in humorous cards for the writer who doesn't mind putting in a lot of time on a single idea. It is not an easy line to write for, and it's certainly not one for which you can expect to whip off thirty or forty ideas a day. Getting good at writing humorous cards takes a certain amount of talent and a good amount of work. You have to familiarize yourself with all the different types of folds, and you have to be constantly on the lookout for new ideas that can be adapted into successful humorous cards.

You'll want to spend a lot of time at greeting card counters becoming acquainted with the kinds of cards that different companies are making. And you'll want to buy a few samples to tear them down and see how they're constructed.

You'll also want to become familiar with humorous captions and themes, as well as with the different kinds of humor formulas covered in this book.

A chapter like this can only scratch the surface of a line as large and diverse as humorous cards. How much you learn is really up to you. It all comes down to studying the cards, writing your own, and learning from your experiences. Eventually those good ideas will begin to take shape.

How to Write
Studio Cards and Still
Have Time Left for Sex

by Bob Hammerquist

You'd like to write studio cards? Well, bless your starry eyes . . . As a card-carrying freelancer, I will now force-feed you with a few of my conclusions about studios, editors, and the System as seen from the wrong side of the New York, New Haven, and Hartford Railroad. Having, for the occasion, through an extraordinary application of willpower on my part, raised the blood content of my Scotch to a preposterous level, I would appreciate your not zonking out for at least a few paragraphs. What I put before you are my own opinions, it is only fair to say, and are not to be confused, necessarily, with reality. However, I have faked my way through this thing for a good number of years now, narrowly missing the almshouse in the process, and this alone, it seems to me, demands a minimal respect on the part of apprentice charlatans.

Compared to the more traditional types of greeting cards, the studio format is still quite new, a mere teenager, but it has been around long enough now to be accepted by most card buyers, dealers, and manufacturers as a reasonably honest American product (which, in case you have never actually seen one in print before, is an authentic lefthanded compliment). The exact birthdate of studios is pretty hazy. They just seemed to appear in the early fifties, coming from any number of small, independent, and somewhat adventurous types who wanted a new way to say Greeting Cards. The huge and near-huge manufacturers at first looked upon the studios as something akin to a New Leftist at the 35th Class Reunion, but the cards' collective health was good, and it seems they may live to a ripe and irreverent old age after all. However, with a prognosis of longevity, and with their present image as a profit maker, 2,850,000 card manufacturers have, as of this date, laid claim to their birth. Yes, studios are here and hearty.

Can you write them? Well, if you're the cool, unflappable, methodical, efficient, reasoning type, I submit that this is not your pasture. You could probably make a go at it, but it would be work.

And it shouldn't be work. It is almost essential that you have a few parts missing . . . or, at least, not functioning properly.

Now, before you jog off in a tricolored snit, please don't dismiss all the advice given you as irrelevant. Throughout this book, and even in this chapter—verily and gasp—there will be a few little dainties it would be good to pay attention to because you just can't get around them. I just don't want you to approach this writing experience (if you'll excuse the expression) wrapped in layers of cumbersome regulations that only work in theory. Read the books, but don't memorize them.

First of all, let's take a look at your sense of humor. Like, have you got one? Of course you do, you say, or you wouldn't be reading this to see how it can be applied. Look coldly at it again. Can you laugh at, or at least appreciate, the different types of humor presented in various situations? Do you like the more sophisticated (yes, I know, thank you, that *is* a relative word) comedians and satirical reviews that zap away at societal shortcomings? And because this is your cup of tea, do you find the average situation comedy inane and beneath your standards? Or is it the other way around? Do you like—and I mean really *like*—sight gags, burlesque, humor, an inflated pig's bladder ricocheting off someone's ear? What about political humor? Religious humor? Ethnic humor? Blue humor? Yes? No? Nice, neat divisions, everything marked GOOD or BAD?

If you plan to write studio cards, and make a few clams at it, it doesn't hurt to appreciate as many styles and types of humor as possible. There are outlets for all of them. Risque ideas or slightly blue material can be either outrageously funny or plain smut masquerading as humor. Satire and parody can be subtle and penetratingly funny. They can also be smug, bitter, self-righteous, and just plain dull. If you understand and like good humor at any level, your job as an idea writer will be that much easier.

Don't Get Discouraged—Part I

No one writer is all things to all editors. Everyone has a flair for writing certain types of material better than others. Some writers have a knack for turning out delicate, whimsical little gems that make me want to cry . . . because I can't do them, except by accident. You know the kind I mean, the delicate as opposed to the boffo, the cute as opposed to the ridiculous. Occasionally we all stumble into an area where we shouldn't be and come up with a nugget, but it's a rarity—to be recognized and capitalized on, nevertheless!

Here are a few examples of the softer-type ideas that I've clubbed into life:

[*outside*]   You've made me see life through different
                   eyes . . .

[*inside*]   [*neuter character with stars as eyes*]

[*outside*]   [*two neuters waving to one another from dif-
                   ferent planets*]
                   Hi . . .!

[*inside*]   How are things in your world?

[*outside*]   [*cute neuter in Halloween costume*]
                   Don't know if I'm a TRICK or a TREAT . . .

[*inside*]   . . . but   I'm all YOURS!

By instinct I am personally from the bedroom/belly button/ bedpan school, and before you look down your freckled beak at that, let me tell you it is rather fun. Simply put, I am betting that bathrooms and bedrooms will be around approximately as long as navels, and that onrushing generations are going to discover, much to their delight, what our peers already know, namely that some very funny things, indeed, do happen in these areas. Not that much really happens in a navel, but what, after all, is a sillier part of the human anatomy? (Well! That's *your* opinion, baby . . . !) And the more you look into it, the sillier it gets. (As my Great Uncle Sigurd once observed . . . a navel doesn't happen, a navel *is!!!* As a matter of fact, he squeaked that one out just seconds before they packed him in ice and shipped him off beyond Chicago somewhere. He seemed happy enough. It worked out well for all of us.) Feast on a few bedroom, belly button, bathroom ideas . . .

[*outside*]   [*man and woman*]
              It's your ANNIVERSARY . . . Don't just
              stand there!

[*inside*]   CONNUBULATE!!
              CONGRATULATIONS!

[*outside*]   Here's how to keep birthdays
              from scaring the PANTS off you . . .

[*inside*]   Fasten them to your BELLY BUTTON!!
              HAPPY BIRTHDAY!

[*outside*]   *For You in the Hospital*
              This card contains no uncouth remarks,
              risque humor, or crude jokes.
              It offers instead a thoughtfully chosen wish to
              comfort and cheer you
              during your hours of restful healing . . .

[*inside*]   . . . May your bedpan always be warm!
              HOPE YOU'RE DOING WELL!

A word of warning: Please, please, please don't flood the market with belly button gags, bedpan gags, or sex gags!!! There is no outstanding shortage in these particular categories, and as you'll see when you read the next chapter, there are plenty of other things to be funny about. But if your bedroom, belly button, or bathroom gag is really a *good* one . . .

Now, please don't sit right down in a creative heat wave and start writing. Not yet. Here comes the advice. Get out where the cards are! Get out to the card racks in the stores and see what's being done. Don't just browse through a few studios you've saved from a couple of years back. Go out and look at the fresh ones until those starry eyes of yours go crossed and your arches go numb. Not just to your favorite or nearby shops, or the ones closest to the liquor store, but to as many and as wide a variety of outlets as you can find—book shops, college shops, variety stores, drugstores, department stores, discount houses, novelty shops, groceries . . . anywhere! You'll find quite a variety in the types of studio cards being sold, from the more reserved (Mmmmm!) to the more earthy (Ah Haa!!!). This may all sound terribly obvious, but the question is—are you going to follow up on it? Get out there! Keep getting out there! There's no better way to find out what studio cards are all about.

Once we're in the store, what are we looking for? No hard-core specifics here, but a few generalities to keep in the back of your mind. First of all: Are they widely sendable? The essential ingredient in any greeting card is SENDABILITY! Four-star important! It has to be sendable . . . it has to relate to a situation! Somebody's having a birthday, remember? Or someone is sick, or is having an anniversary, or is going on a trip, or is a very special type of friend, or is having a toenail transplant. Something pretty specific. The card buyer is in the shop because of one of these or similar reasons, not to see how clever you are at writing zany abstractions— assuming your abstractions would get by the editors, which they would not.

Obviously card buyers want to communicate with people they care for, and they have chosen studio cards because they want to do so in an informal manner. As a writer, you're simply offering them a choice of messages for the communication. Think about this *constantly* when you're writing card material, for any and all occasions . . . birthdays, Christmas, etc. You're *not* writing for a

TV or nightclub comedian, or a comic strip, or for any other medium where anything goes. You're writing studio *greeting cards,* period.

As you write, you might occasionally ask yourself if some unknown person would actually pay out hard-earned cash for this particular idea. Would anyone *steal* it already? Your idea is not standing by itself in the racks—there are hundreds of others lurking about . . . competing! Your idea has to have a number of things in its favor and the most important one is its sendability. Can't get around that.

Here are a few examples of what I would consider very sendable greeting cards:

[*outside*]   Sorry you're so sick!

[*inside*]   Hate to see someone so yummy
                     feeling so crummy!

[*outside*]   Like a vintage wine, we get nicer with
                     age . . .

[*inside*]   . . . though our kegs may be starting to
                     swell . . .
                     HAPPY BIRTHDAY

[*outside*]   *Riddle for Your Birthday*
                     What gets older but looks and acts younger
                     every year??

[*inside*]   HINT:
                     it sleeps in your pajamas . . .
                     HAPPY BIRTHDAY!

Notice that the word "I" doesn't appear in any of these three examples? That's because using the word "I" or "my" limits the number of potential senders of each card to one. It makes the card unsendable by married couples or a whole gang of people. It's not a forbidden word, exactly; plenty of studio cards are sent by individual persons, but it's a word that should be left out unless it's needed. It's a word that limits a card's sendability, and sendability is what a card needs most.

Next consideration—are the cards *clever* or *funny?* Remember, extend your definition of what might conceivably be funny. After all, you're not supposed to cry or be bored stiff . . . you're supposed to laugh.

Here are a few ideas where, hopefully, the emphasis was on *funny*:

[*outside*]	[*woman*] So it's your birthday, and you think you're getting along in years, do you . . . well bless your little heart!
[*inside*]	Sweetie, I've got *girdles* that are older than you!!! HAPPY DAY!
[*outside*]	[*just lettering . . . large and bright:*] BAAOOM!
[*inside*]	Hark! I think you just went through the FOSSIL BARRIER . . . HAPPY BIRTHDAY!
[*outside*]	Congratulations on your success . . . but then, why shouldn't you be successful!?
[*inside*]	You've got more brains in your head than most people have in their little finger!!!

And yet another consideration—are your ideas short and to the point? Most of the good ones are funny (or cute) and as *short* as possible. Very few words—but, hopefully, the right words . . . the ones that move the idea across quickly and smoothly without clouding it up. For the most part, these words don't just happen. They have been selected, judged, trimmed, positioned, invented, etc. For instance:

[*outside*]	I like you . . . you've got smarts!
[*inside*]	Your *sexies* aren't bad, either . . .

[*outside*]	Just a friendly little "Hi!" for your birthday . . .
[*inside*]	. . . 'cause it's cheaper than a friendly little present! HAPPY DAY!

[*outside*]	If you don't like this birthday card, you can exchange it
[*inside*]	. . . for a bloody nose HAPPY BIRTHDAY!

Occasionally, however, you will come up with an idea that seems to be funny enough by itself but in order to make it work as a greeting card, you may have to fabricate a fairly lengthy situation—thusly:

[*outside*]   [*picture of farmer:*] Farmer Ida
[*picture of cow:*] Farmer Ida's cow
As Farmer Cecil Ida said to his dedicated-
but-tired-and-feeble old cow, Bessie Mae,
on the occasion of her twenty-eighth birthday

[*inside*]   . . . HAPPY BIRTHDAY AND NO BULL

[*outside*]   When I heard it was your birthday I went
                        right down to the bank, took out a hundred
                        dollars for your gift, ripped off the
                        wrapper, threw it away, enclosed the cash,
                        sealed the envelope, stamped it, ran to the
                        Post Office and mailed it before anything
                        could go wrong, 'cause you know how I some-
                        times get things fouled up . . .

[*inside*]   [*hundred-dollar bill-wrapper attachment*]
                        HAPPY BIRTHDAY

Length is justified in these cases as a mood, a situation, or a
plausibility is being constructed for the punchline, but if it doesn't
have to be long, don't make it so. Funny and short, if possible!

How do you get ideas? Where do they come from? What's the
secret? Occasionally, someone will ask me this, believe it or not. I
wish there was a secret, but there isn't. No magic techniques. No
polyethylene prayer wheel that spins out the lucky combinations—
you'd have contrived ideas, remember? If you feel a need for max-
ims and do-all devices, maybe you should get into insurance or
banking or something while there are still a few hours left.

Part of the idea-gathering process is simply keeping your eyes
and ears open, and thinking greeting cards twenty-four hours a
day. This isn't to say that you run about like a nut obsessed, salivat-
ing and pulsating, notebook and pencil in hand. They'd put you in
a net. *I'd* put you in a net! No, you go about the business of being
an average, urbane, suave, American All-Star, in complete but
reserved command of all situations. A beautiful person! A sweetheart! But on some secondary level of awareness, you stay constantly awake to all audible and visual funny business. This may
sound like a drag, but, after all, it is a job, and a fun one compared
to many. It's not Sunday afternoon therapy, girls! Look and listen
for the ideas! Simple? Do it, then! TV, radio, movies, theater,

chatter over cocktails and coffee breaks, popular phrases, customs, issues, attitudes and anxieties that reach crests of concern (morality, living costs, etc.), articles and cartoons in magazines and newspapers, and office jokes. These are my humble sources resulting in ideas such as these:

[*outside*]   HOLD IT! ! !
                     Before you light your candles . . .

[*inside*]   . . . did you submit your
                     Environmental Impact Statement??
                     HAPPY BIRTHDAY!

[*outside*]   [*animated rock, singing*]
                     Happy birthday to you . . .
                     Happy birthday to you . . .
                     Happy birthday to you-oo . . .
                     Happy birthday to you!

[*inside*]   Just a little rock music
                     for your birthday . . .

Other greeting cards are also good as idea generators—not to find ideas that you think you can pilfer (although "creative camouflage" is a legitimate part of this business), but as a general stimulant to put you in a frame of mind. Try it, it'll work.

For instance, browsing through the wordplay on other cards prompted me to think of some words that could be broken down into separate and unrelated words that would be so flexible in their combined meaning that almost anything could be read into them:

[*outside*]   Happy Valentine's Day

[*inside*]   . . . to someone who makes my TIDDLY
                               WINK!!!

If you have that sense of humor we've talked about, you can't
help but see and hear those ideas popping up all around you.
People are strange, in case it hasn't come home to you yet. They say
and do wild things by design and accident. They are often beauti-
fully unaware of being funny (aren't we all!). If you're going to
write studio ideas, you have to assume, nitty-gritty-wise, that life is
absurd. You *do* assume that, don't you? It's all a game. There are
altogether too many pompous clowns flapping around who take all
this foolishness seriously.

This is not to say there aren't serious issues or legitimate causes.
Obviously there are glaring, long-standing wrongs to be righted,
but it seems to me that we have an absolute genius for ignoring—or
at least fumbling—the real problems, and making life-and-death
issues out of whether or not we should have 28¼ rather than 28½
acres of tarmac and neon in any given beautification program. I'm
telling you, sweet person, if this society of ours isn't a fountainhead
of gag possibilities, I will personally, and without flinching, hand
you my rubber duck for keepsies.

Living in these United States makes it that much easier to come
up with stuff like this:

[*outside*]   For your Birthday I was going to bake you
                               one of your favorite treats . . .

[*inside*]   . . . but how do you bake beer???
                               HAPPY BIRTHDAY!

[*outside*]   HEY, MOM!
                               For a special Mother's Day treat you get
                               to have breakfast in bed. Just check off
                               what you want from the menu . . .

[*inside*]   [*on homemade menu*]

MENU

Cookies	Chocolate bars
Potato chips	Pepperoni pizza
Pop	Ice cream
Milkshake	French fries

HAPPY MOTHER'S DAY!

[*outside*]   LADIES AND GENTLEMEN . . .
The President of the United States with his
annual Christmas message to the people
regarding the prospects for lower taxes, lower
fuel bills, and less inflation during the
coming year . . .

[*inside*]   HO, HO, HO!
(Merry Christmas!)

All of these idea sources I've described, however, offer very few
ideas directly. By this, I mean the idea that hits you immediately,
and you just know it's a greeting card—and a good one.

For instance, the following ideas came like shots out of the blue—
at different times, of course—when greeting cards were the last
thing on my mind. Zing! There they were. Gifts! No work involved.
No doubt they would sell. Neat, clean, fast—

[*outside*]   Sorry you're laid up . . .
be sure to follow
your doctor's advice, get plenty of rest,
and just to make sure . . .

[*inside*]   Take one of these every 8 hours!
[*small Band-Aid attachment*]

[*outside*]   Granny had a word for birthdays

[*inside*]   The word was "CRAP!"
                    HAPPY DAY

I'm conscious of getting only a small percentage of my ideas via thunderbolts, though—10 percent, maybe 15 percent. Who knows? Who cares?

Now, let me tell you how I really get 'em. The secret! A working day: Rise promptly for breakfast and afterwards lie down and get right to work. If you're the athletic type and have something to prove, you can write sitting up. Gather a few simple tools together: dictionary, thesaurus, paper, and a plastic pencil guaranteed to last 30 words or 30 seconds, whichever comes first. Turn loose. Just think gags and relate them to sendable situations. Some secret, huh? But, if you've done your reading, kept your ears open, been to the card racks, and, indeed, do have a sense of humor, something *has* to happen.

I usually start slow in the morning by running a few old card ideas through my mind. There are always a few favorite cards—words or phrases that stick with you. I do this just to get in first gear. A few variations will develop: strange situations, a popular saying, a couple of words that rhyme, a cute phrase—all of which are atrocious, obvious, and have been done a thousand times by everyone. This might not seem like progress, and maybe it isn't much, but at least it gets the most stagnant thoughts of the day out of the way so as not to waste time with them later.

After this remarkable progression will come a handful or two of slightly more original ideas, mostly bad, with the beginnings of a few definite possibilities. During the early afternoon, usually a couple of dozen partially developed ideas are bouncing around, and maybe ten or twelve definites are put on ice. I'll add a few new possibilities, rewrite some of the previous ones, and during the last part of the afternoon, everything somehow starts falling into place and completed ideas will come in clusters. At the end of a full day, there should be between forty and fifty intact ideas. I read them all over immediately and chop out about a half a dozen of the very worst, not throwing them away, however, because even from this compost heap something can occasionally be salvaged.

The next morning, I read the whole batch through again. Opinions of more than a few will definitely have changed during the night! Maybe a dozen more ideas will be eliminated. So I will have thirty or so ideas to show for the previous day's work. If I'm not working on a definite assignment with a specific deadline, I put these ideas away for a week or two before reading them over once again. The last checkover!

It's easy to overdo this reviewing business, and there is a tendency to rewrite the very life out of an idea if you look at it long enough. I'd still advise, though, to let those hot ideas and that simmering head cool off for a few days before making final decisions about which ideas to send out. I guarantee that you will be horror-stricken with some of your creations. I still suffer from an uncontrollable twitching in the presence of my ever-mounting supply of rejects. The ones that have come home to die.

Pure twaddle! I've done everything wrong there is to do, and I continue to do it on a certain percentage of cards. Look, they can't all be jewels. We do the best we can, pal, and that's it! The objective is to not waste the editor's time with *all* your worst efforts. Remember, they have their own hang-ups to untangle, and have only so much time to devote to you personally and to greeting cards in general.

On a writing day, then, I shoot for thirty or forty ideas. If they're *everyday* ideas, about 60-65 percent will eventually make it into print. *(Editor's note:* This figure is probably higher than what a normal writer should expect to achieve, but then, no one ever accused Hammerquist of being normal.) For certain *seasonal* stuff, like Christmas ideas, the percentage will be lower. Not all of these ideas will be sold in the highest-paying markets during the first two weeks. It may take quite a while—but remember, somewhere, is an editor or publisher with a fat wallet and a printing deadline to meet. If you give him an honest effort, your chances are pretty good.

I'm sure there are some hot hands that would pshaw at thirty or forty ideas per day as a goal. They really crank them out! And I'm sure there are many (especially part-timers) who will be satisfied with half that output. Quantity is *not* the name of the game! What's the sense of turning them out by the hundreds if they don't stand a chance of selling? Even I couldn't come up with thirty or forty ideas a day, five days a week, week after week. It could be done for a while, but things just have to get stale after a bit. Ask any horse. The point is, set yourself a realistic goal and strive to reach it.

Fortunately, you will not have to sustain your creative energies full-time. When you have a few hundred ideas going, you will spend more than a little time keeping records of where they are, who has bought what, who needs what, and when. If you're inefficient, which you'll remember was a prerequisite of being a studio card writer, you will never have enough stamps or envelopes, and the typewriter ribbon will always be in sideways. When you get a few thousand ideas going, confusion escalates. Naturally, you will also spend three or four days a month just hauling sacks of money to the bank.

All of these little time-consumers are part of running a small business, and, although boring, they at least make you eager to get back to writing—and that's the way you should come to it. Even when you pace your writing, you'll turn out lemons. It's unavoidable. Don't worry about them. They are marginal ideas you're not quite sure of: you're just about positive that they're bad, but there's a lingering doubt. So you send them off.

Another little involvement that can eat up hours is artwork. This can work to your advantage or disadvantage, depending on how proficient you are at drawing or sketching. If you honestly feel you have no talent in this area, just type out your ideas plain. If they're good, they'll sell. After all, that's what it's all about—ideas! If, however, you like to sketch little comic figures, or the neuter, simple characters you see on so many studio cards, and can do it quickly, fine. It can't hurt. This type of artwork will not turn a bad idea into a good one, but it can put any idea into a more impressive package.

What value this has, everything else being equal, is debatable. It's up to you. However, if you decide to use simple illustrations, study those little characters when you go out to look over cards. At first glance, they appear very elementary, and a great many *are* neuter, sex-wise, but look closely at those facial expressions, body positions, gestures of arms, legs, shoulders, eyelids, mouth, fingers, etc. These little figures are happy, or sad, or confused, or angelic, or bitter, or excited, or fatigued, or serene, or just about anything depending on the gist of the idea. They back up the idea. They're in harmony with it.

If you can't quickly sketch the right expression or gesture, but, on the contrary, consistently turn out vapid, lifeless characters, or, worse yet, characters with the wrong expressions, they can only fight the ideas, not help them. However, at this point in the development of a card, the artwork is just not that important. Don't get hung up on it.

Don't Get Discouraged—Part II

Rejection slips! PHHHhhht! I have mine made into suits, and what's left over, I sell to paper junkies at a nickel a ton. These slips read, in spite of the fact that they're not intended to, like the final deathblow. They're not as cold as they look. Editors simply don't have the time to write consoling, explanatory little notes. Find a good tailor or dressmaker.

Don't Get Discouraged—Part III

Almost all editors have certain types of ideas they do not want to see, but what is not wanted varies from editor to editor. No sex stuff, please! No bedpan or belly button gags! No topical ideas! No trick folds! No brand names! No too-cutesy-pie. No whatever! You may wonder occasionally if there is anything left. Well, if you can relate it to a sendable situation, and get it to the *right* company, you can sell it. Different companies have an image to maintain or protect, or, for one reason or another, they have found that certain types of ideas just do not sell in their particular line. They know what they're doing. (Except, of course, the ones who have folded in the past few years. Hoo-ha!)

If an editor states he doesn't want to see a particular type of idea, don't keep throwing it in his face, or give him advice about his unimaginative approach to publishing. They have their different markets and they know as well as anyone what sells in them. Occasionally you can slip in a taboo subject or two, just to see if anyone is paying attention. Companies have been known, on rare occasions, to change their editorial viewpoints. As a freelancer, you've got to keep probing. Just don't push too hard. You will quickly learn that each company has a distinct personality of its own and that if you channel the right idea to the right company, very few subjects or approaches are unsalable.

For instance, here is a studio idea that *had* to go to the right type of company. It would have been a waste of everyone's time to send it out indiscriminately:

[*outside*]   Happy Mother's Day, Mom dear . . .
and although I don't usually talk this way,
I want you to know I think you're . . .

[*inside*]   . . . one helluva nice MOTHER!

The problem word is "helluva," and it's the basis for the whole idea; but there are a few companies that wouldn't touch this type of thing, even though it would have to be classified as a "cute" idea.

A word about integrity. I know you're honest, but you worry about some of those big companies and what they do with your precious, unprotected ideas, right? The honesty of the companies, as well as of yourself, should be dictated, if not by sheer morality, at least by common sense. They are *not* going to make copies of your ideas or artwork and return the originals to you with a rejection slip. If you feed them junk, they wouldn't want to steal it even if they were bandits. If you're valuable to them as a contributor, they want to keep you happy. Trust them! (Trust me!) They play a perfectly honest game of ball, both the large and small companies. The checks are good and usually quite prompt.

In return, you don't play hanky-panky with ideas, naturally. The editors and their cohorts who check over your ideas know pretty much what this game is all about. They have a built-in sensitivity to most ideas that have been used before, in their particular line as well as in other lines. As mentioned before, borrowing an idea from a source other than greeting cards and converting it to a card situation is not exactly plagiarism, you understand, but borrowing from another greeting card without giving it an original twist of your own is something else again. Use some old-fashioned common sense. If an idea looks at all like trouble, drop it quickly. Get on to one that's positive.

The future of studio cards, along with the future of greeting cards in general, looks good, but why, I'll never know. I suppose it is simply easier to send words written and printed by someone else than it is to sit down and write a note personally. After all, if you can't communicate orally, or for some reason choose not to, it would seem that a handwritten note would be a more sincere way to do it. So who has the time or the talent to do things right? A few still do, I'm told, but not many.

So we have greeting cards, and in my world they fall into two categories—*studios* and *others*—and to me, the *others* don't make it. I'm talking about cards for adults, now. Juvenile cards are in a class by themselves. To some extent, I represent the fans who have grown up with studios, and there are more followers coming along all the time. The sweet, lengthy verses of the *others* are simply a bit much. To be sure, they make up the greatest part of the industry today—probably will forever—and, obviously, they have their legions who lap them up, but to each his own, Hirschel. The pack I run with simply feel that for someone else to state our feelings of concern in the form of a sweet little poem—not to be confused with poetry—for us to buy and send is a bit slick.

On the other hand, we won't write those intimate little notes, either. We settle for studio cards. It's a cop-out to the personal touch, but we can live with it. It's a less traditional, less pretentious way of saying the same old things. This doesn't mean we have to be sarcastic, irreverent, or risqué—although we can be. We can also be cute, sweet, whimsical, just plain nice, without making a production out of it. Studios are like the people who enjoy sending and receiving them: the young and those who think young (or think they do, anyhow). A little more direct, uncluttered, and candid, but not way, way out or completely demented—like so:

[*outside*]   Another birthday!?

[*inside*]   Well, bless your brittle bones . . .
                 HAPPY DAY!!!

[*outside*]   On your birthday . . . no ill-conceived re-
                 marks about candle-laden cakes, or ine-
                 briated celebrations, or midriff expansion
                 or such; just a simple wish I hope you'll find
                 refreshing.

[*inside*]   May your cesspool never clog.

[*outside*]   Happy Birthday to a typical red-blooded
                 American guy!

[*inside*]   32% warm blood . . . 68% cold beer . . .

[*outside*]   [*inebriated Santa, burping*]
                 UUUuuuuuurrrrrppp!

[*inside*]   . . . and his reindeer are made out of
                 plastic . . .

To wind it up, then: Don't make a fetish out of looking for
formulas to follow and rules to remember that will guarantee the
perfect ideas every time. Let the editors do the heavy worrying
about such matters. They're better at it than we are. Part of their
job, after all, is to make those final, nasty, tight decisions. Our job is
to give them as wide and effective a choice as possible. As idea
people, we're in at the very beginning of a greeting card, and this is
no time to pussyfoot. Unwind! Throw a few curves! Zingers!

Tempered—of course, and, ahem—with a little bit of common sense, restraint, and self-editing. But not too much.

Remember, you're not a machine, you're *you*. No one else! Big deal, you say? Yet, some people tend to forget this. They try to wear the bag the way others have worn it before. Come on now, that's not going to do it—you know that! For those *original* ideas, it comes back to *you* alone. *Your* viewpoints. It's really the only thing you've got that nobody else has.

If you decide to give it a go, I'll tell you the *real* story when we meet in person, maybe at the post office, as you send off a batch of money-makers. You'll recognize me. I'll be the one standing out front on the sidewalk—wrapped in a horse blanket—selling used plastic pencils.

Things
to Be
Funny About

by Larry Sandman

Now that you have some idea of *how* to write funny cards, let's take a look at *what* most greeting card editors want you to be funny about. What will it mean, for instance, if an editor sends you a market letter (needs list) that says, "Need Wedding Anniversary, General, Wish, Non-risqué," or "Need General Birthday, Gift Gags . . . Get Well, Doctor Gags . . ."? In this chapter we'll cover the major captions and themes used in studio and humorous lines.

Like other types of cards, studio and humorous cards can be divided into two distinct lines—*everyday* cards and *seasonal* cards. Everydays are those cards which can be sent on any day of the year—for example, *birthday, get well, anniversary,* and *friendship* cards. Seasonals are, as the name suggests, cards that are sent at special seasons like *Valentine's Day, Easter,* and *Christmas.* Seasonals are sometimes called *holiday* lines.

Not all companies publish cards for both lines. Several publish only everyday cards. Some publish nothing but Christmas cards. You will also find that most of the major card companies produce everyday studio and humorous lines that are considerably larger than their seasonal lines. This usually translates into bigger opportunities for the freelance writer in the everyday lines. As a writer it's important that you be up on what each company is producing and on what each of your editors needs. Always find out what seasonal cards your editor is looking for before you submit. Sending the wrong cards at the wrong time wastes both your editor's time and your own. Some companies have open-door policies by which they'll review ideas for any season at any time. But many companies have specific times for reviewing certain seasons, captions, or themes. A simple query about the editor's needs will keep you informed, and in this business, it pays to be informed!

The first of our two general divisions, the *everyday line,* can be broken down into several categories, including birthday, get well (or illness), friendship, anniversary, wedding, congratulations, and travel cards. There will be variations from company to company in the names used and in the way these titles are classified. For instance, travel cards might be included in the friendship category by some companies. The listings are really rather arbitrary. What is important is that most of the same card-sending-situation ideas are needed by all the major companies, with the exception of a few fringe needs like diet cards or apologies.

Within these everyday categories are many *captions*. Captions are the designations that tell us who a particular card will be sent to or by. A "female" or "feminine" caption, for instance, means that the card is meant to be sent to a woman, and a "male" or "masculine" caption means it is to be sent to a man.

Since the *birthday* category is far and away the largest category, it should come as no surprise that it has the greatest number of captions. Approximately half of all cards sold in the everyday line are birthday cards. The smart writer will plan his efforts accordingly.

In this chapter we will give listings of the major caption areas in the everyday and seasonal lines for both studio and humorous cards. Later in the chapter we'll give examples as we further divide our lines into "themes." Here is a list of *studio birthday* captions:

General (accounts for about one-half of cards in this category)
Female/Feminine
Male/Masculine
From Both
From Group
Relative (a few major companies have specific family titles such as wife, sister, etc.; most buy only general relative cards)

A list of *humorous birthday* captions would include the same titles, and might also include:

Across the Miles	Pop
Our Wishes	Mother from Both

Secret Pal	Dad from Both
Special Friend	Daughter
Honey	Daughter-In-Law
Sweetheart	Son
Wife	Son-In-Law
Husband	Sister
Hubby	Sis
Better-Half	Sister-In-Law
Mother	Brother
Mom	Brother-In-Law
Dad	Cousin

Illness or *get well* cards make up an important part of both the studio and humorous lines, a part that is becoming more and more important as the number of older people in our society inches up. Here are the most common *studio illness* captions:

General
Feminine
Masculine
Hospital (may also include specific masculine and feminine
    cards)
Operation
Accident
From Group/All

Humorous illness captions are the same as studio, with the addition of From Both.

Another major caption area in studio cards is *friendship*. Friendship is somewhat of a catchall category that includes all of the captions that don't appear in the birthday, illness, wedding, anniversary, or congratulations categories. A list of *studio friendship* captions includes:

General
Miss You
Sorry Haven't Written

Please Write
Thank You
Diet
Travel/Trip
Goodbye

Many of these captions could be listed as individual categories. General and Miss You are the most important captions in this group. Many companies do not carry diet, travel, or goodbye cards. If in doubt, check with your editor.

The *humorous friendship* lines of most companies are rather small. Most friendship needs are covered through the companies' special promotions—groups of twelve or more cards on a common theme, of which usually at least half, sometimes all, are friendship (see Chapter 13—"Creating and Selling Promotions"). Humorous friendship captions are the same as studio captions.

The *studio anniversary* category includes:

General (with no reference to wedding)
Wedding
Our Wedding

The same captions are used for *humorous anniversary* cards, along with:

Wife
Husband
Hubby
Better-Half
Mother and Dad

Both *studio wedding* and *humorous wedding* are very small categories, sharing the captions of General and From Both.

The *studio congratulations* and *humorous congratulations* categories also share the same basic captions:

General
Baby (some studio and most humorous lines include specific
    captions for baby girl or baby boy)
Retirement
New Home

Many lines also carry one or more of the following congratulations captions:

New Car
Promotion
New Apartment

The *seasonal* lines of most companies do not have many different captions. Most studio lines stick to General captions with occasional appearances of Wife, Husband, From Both, or From All/Group. Mother/Mom and Father/Dad appear in Mother's Day and Father's Day, respectively.

The humorous lines carry any of the following captions, depending on the company and season:

General (found in most all companies that make humorous seasonal cards, and in every season)
Secret Pal (carried through all seasons by those companies who use this caption)
Across the Miles
Our Wishes
From Both
Special Friend
Honey
Sweetheart
Wife/Husband
Hubby
Better-Half
Mother
Mom
Mother From Both
Dad
Pop
Dad From Both
Daughter
Son
Sister
Sis
Brother

Major seasons like Christmas and Valentine's Day will find many companies carrying most all of these captions. Lesser seasons like Thanksgiving and St. Patrick's Day will see the captions dwindle to a very few. Of course, feminine captions are used in Mother's Day cards and masculine captions at Father's Day.

Seasons and special days for which studio and humorous cards commonly appear include:

New Year's
Valentine's Day
St. Patrick's Day
Easter
April Fool's Day
Mother's Day
Graduation
Father's Day
Halloween
Thanksgiving
Christmas

Now that we've covered the main captions used in humorous and studio lines, and we have a pretty good idea of *who* we'll be writing the cards for, let's take a look at what subjects or *themes* we can write about.

There are several popular themes in studio and humorous greeting cards, some of which appear over and over in different captions. Some themes—compliments, for example—are so universally well liked that they appear, not only in all seasons, but in all types of cards—studio, humorous, conventional, juvenile, informal, etc. Other themes, like sex, for instance, are limited to studio, occasional humorous, or promotional usage, and then only in certain situations.

Themes are very important in humorous and studio cards, because they're one of the classifications by which most editors break down their lines. Keeping a proper balance of compliments, wishes, drinking gags, sex gags, and such, is one of an editor's most important jobs. It's the only way he can be sure that his line will appeal to all the different kinds of people who buy studio or humorous cards. And since themes are so important to editors, they should also be important to writers, for if you can write to an editor's needs, you have a much better chance of selling your idea than does the writer who counts on luck.

Since birthday cards make up about half of the everyday line, and since general birthday cards make up about half of the total number of birthday cards, it's no surprise that the largest number of themes appear in the general birthday caption.

The simplest, most direct birthday theme is a *wish*. Here's a typical example of a wish-type sentiment:

[*outside*]   [*photo: giraffe*]
                 High . . .

[*inside*]   HAPPY BIRTHDAY!

The wish is probably the most sendable of all studio and humorous themes, and it's closely followed by *compliments*. A complimentary card can be direct, or it can be more tongue in cheek, like this one:

[*outside*]   Don't think you're so darn young and
                 good-looking and smart . . .

[*inside*]   . . . just because you're so darn young and
                 good-looking and smart!
                 HAPPY BIRTHDAY

Compliments can be directed to the sender rather than the receiver, or, better yet, to both, as in these examples:

[*outside*]   You're such a warm, intelligent,
                 attractive person . . .

[*inside*]   If you weren't you, I'd swear
                 you were me!
                 HAPPY BIRTHDAY!

[*outside*]   Blessed are the young and good-looking . . .

[*inside*]   . . . for we shall be worshipped and envied
                       by all!
                       HAPPY BIRTHDAY!

Closely related to compliments are the mild insults or *slams* that
sort of say, "You know I like you, but you're never going to get me
to admit it!" Here's a typical *mild slam:*

[*outside*]   [*art: frog*]
                       You get wiser, wittier, and sexier
                       with every birthday!

[*inside*]   You've just heard from the birthday
                       BULLfrog!
                       HAVE A WONDERFUL DAY!

One of the bestselling themes in birthday cards has always been
the *age gags*. They can take the form of straight gags:

[*outside*]   Don't get discouraged because you think
                       old age is creeping up on you . . .

[*inside*]   . . . it may just be tight underwear!
                       HAPPY BIRTHDAY!

They can take the form of age slams:

[*outside*]   This wish isn't new . . .

[*inside*]   But, then, neither are you!
                       HAPPY BIRTHDAY!

Or they can take the form of age compliments:

[*outside*]   *Riddle for Your Birthday:*
                       What gets older but looks and acts
                       younger every year??

[*inside*]   HINT:
                    It sleeps in your pajamas . . .
                    HAPPY BIRTHDAY!

Gift gags are a natural theme for birthday cards, whether they
are about a special gift—

[*outside*]   For your Birthday, I've got this
                    fantastic trained bird that will sit on your
                    head and sing Happy Birthday to you . . .

[*inside*]   . . . I'm afraid to tell you what he does for an
                    encore!
                    HAPPY BIRTHDAY!

—or whether they are saying, "Sorry I don't have a gift for you":

[*outside*]   I would have gotten you
                    a nice Birthday present . . .

[*inside*]   [*art: character peering out of die-cut hole*]
                    . . . but I'm a little in the hole right now!
                    HAPPY BIRTHDAY, ANYWAY

Sometimes the card is offered quite unashamedly in place of a gift:

[*outside*]   HAPPY BIRTHDAY!
                    Let's run down what I got you in
                    alphabetical order . . .

[*inside*]   A
                    B irthday
                    C ard

Money that never quite makes it into the receiver's hand has long
been a standard in the gift gags:

[*outside*]   For your Birthday I was going to send you
                    ten dollars . . . but then I thought, you're
                    worth a HUNDRED dollars!

[*inside*]   . . . and I didn't have a hundred dollars,
                     so I forgot the whole thing!
                     HAPPY BIRTHDAY ANYWAY!

Drinking has also been a longtime standard in studio and humorous cards. Here's a representative sample of a drinking card:

[*outside*]   A BIRTHDAY DRINK-O-METER
                     EXHALE ON THIS SPOT
                     [*green spot*]
                     If it turns red, you've had enough to drink!

[*inside*]   If it doesn't, your card is broken!
                     HAPPY BIRTHDAY!

It isn't easy to come up with a drinking gag that is different enough to sell to an editor today, but it does happen. Here's one that was purchased recently:

[*outside*]   I knew you were someone special
                     the very first time I saw you! . . .

[*inside*]   I think it was the beer foam on your nose
                     and the pretzel hanging from your ear!

Notice that beer is the subject of this drinking gag. A large percentage of drinking gags being purchased by editors today are beer gags. It has really seemed to surpass the martini or the screwdriver in universal appeal.

If there is any one subject in which studio cards have really stood apart from all other types of greeting cards it is in the use, in the studio lines, of *suggestive* humor. When we say "suggestive," most of us immediately think of the risque, sex-oriented type of card. That has certainly been a part of most studio lines, in one form or another. Sex, as a greeting card theme, is treated differently by different companies, however, and it would be to the writer's advantage to go to the trouble to determine which company is interested in what. None of the major companies are interested in smut, but some are more liberal than others in what they will accept. Most companies would be willing to print something along the line of the following example (and, in fact, most companies already have!):

[outside]   [*two monkeys with arms around each other*]
                   On your birthday,
                         let's get together . . .

[inside]   . . . and monkey around!

Of course, "monkey around" can be taken as innocently or as naughtily as you like. This is a "safe" card, one that would have a good chance of selling if everyone didn't have some version of it already.

There is one way to play it safe on the sex subject, while possibly squeezing a few more bucks out of it. That way is the *risque/non-risque* card, the kind of card that starts out as though it's gonna be dirty, but ends with a very innocent, and hopefully funny, twist. Here's a good example of risque/non-risque:

[outside]   It's your BIRTHDAY! And it's also your
                   chance to take part in this important survey.
                   (Just circle your answer to the question be-
                   low.)

                   HOW DO YOU FEEL AFTER YOU DO
                            IT?

                   A. Relaxed and kind of tingly all over.
                   B. Charged up and ready for more.
                   C. Exhausted and feel like going to
                      sleep . . .

[inside]   . . . or haven't you ever blown out ALL
                   your candles before?
                   HAPPY BIRTHDAY!

Related to the sex theme is another branch of suggestive cards, the nudity gag:

[*outside*]	Want to be MASSAGED, STROKED, RUBBED, CARESSED, and TITILLATED on your birthday?!!
[*inside*]	. . . Run naked through a car wash! HAVE A HAPPY BIRTHDAY!

There is also a place among the suggestive cards for mild profanity, as long as it's cleverly done, and not just vulgarity for vulgarity's sake. Here's a card that uses profanity, but in a light treatment that's meant to tickle rather than offend:

[*outside*]	[*little devil*] Hi!
[*inside*]	Howthehellareya?

Toilet humor is categorized by some companies under the suggestive theme, perhaps because it, like the other suggestive cards, must walk a tight line. Toilet humor should be light, usually silly in tone—never gross or vulgar. Here's a toilet humor idea that stays well within most people's limitations for good taste:

[*outside*]	Knowing you're someone who appreciates culture, this birthday card was chosen for you because it has a special French touch . . .
[*inside*]	. . . a poodle oui-ouied on it! HAPPY BIRTHDAY!

Related to the suggestive cards, but usually more widely sendable, are those whose message is "Have a good time on your birthday—just get out and *celebrate!*" Here's a good-selling card with a celebrate theme:

[*outside*]	It's your Birthday,

so be good!
Have fun!

[*inside*]   . . . the choice is yours!
                     HAPPY BIRTHDAY!

Many companies have one or more birthday cards on a *sports* theme. The theme may vary, but it's usually on a major spectator or participation sport like football, golf, or bowling. Here's an example of a sports card that uses tennis:

[*outside*]   [*tennis player*]
                     HAPPY BIRTHDAY!

[*inside*]   . . . and many happy returns!

And here's one that features golf:

[*outside*]   Old golfers never die . . .

[*inside*]   . . . they just improve their lie!
                     HAPPY BIRTHDAY, SWINGER!

Another form of humor that is found mostly in the studio line, and sometimes in humorous, is *topical* humor—gags about things that are happening in our world today. Here's an idea based on the oil shortage:

[*outside*]   Due to the energy shortage, your birthday
                     party has been cancelled . . .

[*inside*]   . . . hell, what's a birthday party if you
                     can't get gassed up.

Besides being topical, it's a drinking gag with a mild profanity. Keep in mind, when referring to a listing like this, that few cards are pure this or pure that. It is a general theme that your editor is concerned with, and you shouldn't bother yourself with other little aspects of a gag that pop up unless your editor has given you specific instructions about subthemes.

Some ideas are so unusual that they seem to defy classification. We editors, being what we are, have to attach names to everything. Here's an idea that might be classified, for lack of a better answer, as a *joke* card. It is basically a joke that has been adapted to a greeting card. Editors don't generally write out million-dollar advances for writers to come up with unclassifiable sentiments, but if they come across one that's really good . . .

[*outside*]	Because it's your birthday, I consulted my ouija board . . .
[*inside*]	. . . it said that you'll live for 316 years, be reincarnated as a eucalyptus tree in eastern Java, and be cut down to build an outhouse.
	p.s. It also said that you'll have a HAPPY BIRTHDAY!

Masculine and feminine captioned birthday cards utilize many of the same themes as the generals, such as *wishes, compliments, age angles,* and *gift gags.* Here's a couple of masculine cards that have a *mild slam* and *sex* as their respective themes:

[*outside*]	Happy Birthday to a man who's rugged, handsome, virile . . .
[*inside*]	. . . and a little whacko!

[*outside*]	HEY, BIG BOY, Bet I know what you want for your Birthday . . .
[*inside*]	. . . but you'll have to settle for this card and a cold shower! HAPPY BIRTHDAY!

And here are two feminine cards that use *age* and *compliment* themes:

[*outside*] You're 29, dearie? I'll buy that . . .

[*inside*] I'll buy *anything* that's been reduced!
HAPPY BIRTHDAY!

[*outside*] HAPPY BIRTHDAY . . .

[*inside*] . . . from one sweet young thing to another!
AND MANY HAPPY RETURNS!

The main point to keep in mind when writing for small categories like Group Birthday, or Birthday From Both captions is sendability. *Wishes* or *compliments* tend to be the most widely sendable cards, and so these themes are the most likely candidates for small captions. Here's a group card that uses a direct *wish:*

[*outside*] [*bunch of animated bananas*]
HAPPY BIRTHDAY

[*inside*] . . . from the whole bunch!

Many general relative birthday cards use "family tree" approaches such as this:

[*outside*] *To a Special Relative*
No one could ever take your place
on our family tree!

[*inside*] . . . (not that we've been looking or anything!)
HAPPY BIRTHDAY!

Mild, nonmalicious *slams* like this are common in general relatives and are sometimes found in humorous specific family captions like brother and sister. *Compliments* are more common, though, and, in the studio line especially, there are many cases like the following example in which the compliment is shared by the sender and receiver:

[*outside*]   Isn't it amazing that we're related?

[*inside*]   . . . all that intelligence and good looks in one family!
HAPPY BIRTHDAY!

Belated birthday cards often grow out of the appropriate theme of *forgetfulness:*

[*outside*]   I have a very good reason for forgetting your birthday . . .

[*inside*]   . . . but I forget what it was!
(Hope your day was happy!)

"Sorry I forgot" is a common expression in belated cards as well. Here's an example of what might be termed an *apology* theme card:

[*outside*]   [*jackass speaking*]
Sorry I missed your birthday . . .

[*inside*]   I feel like such a human!
BELATED HAPPY BIRTHDAY!

Having special themes of their own doesn't rule out the use of more common themes. Many belated cards use *compliments, wishes,* or *drinking* themes on their way to saying a belated happy birthday.

Studio and humorous illness cards use many of the themes that are found in birthday cards, such as *wishes, compliments, drinking gags, suggestive* ideas, and occasionally *gift gags.* Here's a general illness card that is built around a short, pleasant *wish.* It simply says:

[*outside*]   Get well soon . . .

[*inside*]   . . . for heaven's sake!

The artwork features, of course, an angel. At the other extreme is a *drinking* card that reads:

[*outside*]   You'd never be sick if you took a shot of bourbon
                    before going to bed each night
                    like I do . . .

[*inside*]   . . . in fact, sometimes I go to bed
                    five or six times a night!
                    GET WELL SOON!

In addition, illness cards have some themes of their own. *Doctor gags* have been popular for many years. Here are two good approaches to the doctor gag theme—the "doctor getting rich off of you" angle and the "quack doctor" approach:

[*outside*]   Don't worry about a thing!
                    Your doctor keeps up with all the latest journals!

[*inside*]   . . . Wall Street Journal
                    . . . Investment Journal
                    . . . Swiss Banking Journal
                    GET WELL SOON

[*outside*]   I don't know what those doctors
                    are talking about???

[*inside*]   You don't look like a guinea pig!
                    GET WELL SOON

Illness, operation, and hospital cards also have their own special themes, including *hospital food, nurse gags, hypodermic needle gags,* and *hospital bed gags.* These captions can also use *compliments, wishes, drinking gags, suggestive humor,* and, of course, *doctor gags:*

[*outside*]   Don't worry about your operation . . .
                        Your doctor has a perfect track record . . .

[*inside*]   . . . last week he saved *twelve horses!*
                        GET WELL SOON!

Accident cards do not have quite as wide a range of themes, partly because we tend to want to be not too hard on someone who's just had an accident. *Compliments* are especially nice for this caption. *Wishes* and clever *gift gags* work, too. Here's a simple, not very funny, but nicely sendable *complimentary* accident card:

[*outside*]   Accidents happen to the nicest people . . .

[*inside*]   . . . you certainly proved that!
                        HOPE YOU GET WELL SOON!

The possibilities for themes for general friendship cards are practically endless, and to try to list them all would be folly. Friendships could range from a simple *hello* themed card such as:

[*outside*]   [*funny-looking pig*]
                        Hi!

[*inside*]   How's it goink?

to a very *romantic*:

[*outside*]   I feel I'm close to perfection . . .

[*inside*]   . . . when I'm close to you!

to a rather *slammish*:

[*outside*]   We'll be friends forever . .

[*inside*]   . . . if you don't louse it up!

to a zany *suggestive*:

[*outside*]   NOTICE: This card can only be opened by
                   VIRGINS . . .
                   [*card is glued shut*]

[*on back*]   . . . I couldn't open it either!

Friendship cards could, depending on the caption, use any theme common to birthday cards, except perhaps for *age angles*— and I suppose there's some incredible writer out there who could use *them,* though Lord knows why he'd want to try!

Specific captions in friendships often dictate what the most appropriate themes might be. Please-write cards often use *mild slams* or even obviously phony *threats.* Sorry-I-haven't-written cards call for *apologies, excuses,* and *sender slams.* Miss You cards may be *complimentary* or simple *thoughts;* some, but not all, should be *romantic.*

Wedding and wedding anniversary cards are particularly well suited for *wishes,* or for *compliments* such as this:

[*outside*]   This is an extra-special wedding card . . .

[*inside*]   . . . because it's for an extra-special couple!
                   CONGRATULATIONS AND BEST
                   WISHES!

The *sex* theme is natural for this category, as it is used here:

[*outside*]   *A Wedding Gift from Both of Us.*
                   Here's something to help insure
                   a happy beginning for your marriage.

[*inside*]   . . . just cut it out and hang on your door-
                   knob!!

                   PLEASE DO NOT DISTURB!!!

                   Congratulations!

Keep in mind that not all wedding and wedding anniversary cards should have *sex* themes. There are many situations in which it would be awkward at best to send such a card. Alternatives should be available, mostly in the forms of *wishes* and *compliments.*

Wishes and *compliments* are also in order for the many types of congratulations cards; such simple, direct sentiments as:

[*outside*]   Congratulations . . .

[*inside*]   You done good!

and:

[*outside*]   You're Retiring . . .

[*inside*]   . . . couldn't happen to a nicer person!

may not be the funniest ideas you've ever read, but they're good sellers, better sellers than many cards that are funnier but not as widely sendable.

When you switch over into the *seasonal* captions you will find that many of the themes from everyday captions can be taken along. *Wishes* and *compliments* are always good. There's never a bad season for saying "I like you," and "I wish you happiness." Other themes, too, can be carried over from everyday into appropriate seasons, such as *gift gags* for Christmas and *drinking gags* for St. Patrick's Day. In addition, each holiday has some themes that are traditionally associated with the season.

Valentine's Day is traditionally a holiday for lovers. It's a time for saying such things as:

[*outside*]   Happy Valentine's Day to the nicest wife
                   a man could ask for!

[*inside*]   . . . from the man who's glad he asked!

Ironically, it's also an occasion for *slams* like this one:

[*outside*]   I would have sent you a VALENTINE
                   more in keeping with your social status,
                   cultural background, life style, and artistic
                   tastes . . .

[*inside*]   . . . but the 25¢ ones were all sold out!
                      HAPPY VALENTINE'S DAY!

Suggestive valentines such as the next example are also widely
used:

[*outside*]   [*written all over cover*]
                      KISS! SMACK! SMOOCH!
                 SMACKO! SMUCK! KISSEY POO!!

[*inside*]   . . . and that's just what I can do with my
                      lips!!!
                      HAPPY VALENTINE'S DAY!

St. Patrick's Day calls for *blarney stone gags, leprechauns, drinking, being Irish,* and an occasional *suggestive* idea, like this one:

[*outside*]   For more fun on St. Patrick's Day
                      wear this . . .

[*inside*]   [*on punch-out badge*]
                      OFFICIAL SHILLELAGH INSPECTOR

                      Happy St. Patrick's Day!

Here's a particularly nice *compliment* for St. Patrick's Day:

[*outside*]   Sure 'n you're the kind of person . . .

[*inside*]   . . . who keeps Irish eyes smilin'
                      HAPPY ST. PATRICK'S DAY!

Easter is a season symbolized by *rabbits, eggs, Easter bonnets,*
and *flowers.* All these things are potential card themes. *Love* is a
good theme, as are the ever-present *wishes* and *compliments.* A
compliment and a mild *slam* combine to make up this Easter sentiment:

[*outside*]   Easter Greetings to someone
                      who's a real good egg!

[*inside*]   . . . a little cracked, maybe,
                   but a good egg!
                   HAPPY EASTER!

You might think that *toilet humor* is out of place at Easter, but here's a successful Easter card that says a lot about when not to give up in your search for new ways to apply old themes:

[*outside*]   The Easter bunny will be hiding
                   lots of surprises around your place—
                   colored eggs, jelly beans, chocolate
                   bunnies . . .
                   but watch out . . .

[*inside*]   . . . the little brown ones aren't
                   chocolate-covered raisins!!!
                   HAPPY EASTER!

Mother's Day and Father's Day share a lot of themes with the everyday captions, perhaps because they are holidays built around people, just as birthdays are. *Love, gratitude, compliments, wishes,* and *jokes* about everyday life are appropriate for these days. Here's a clever *complimentary* card for Mother's Day:

[*outside*]   Mother, I'm writing you a poem for
                   Mother's Day . . .

[*inside*]   What rhymes with wonderful?
                   HAPPY MOTHER'S DAY WITH LOVE!

Here's another where the *compliment* is shared by the sender:

[*outside*]   A mother as special as you
                   deserves the very best!

[*inside*]   . . . guess that's why you got me!
                   HAPPY MOTHER'S DAY!

Graduation is open to many themes, among them *congratulations, wishes, compliments, gift gags, drinking gags, celebrate,* and mild *slams,* like the following:

[*outside*]   CONGRATULATIONS, GRADUATE!
                 You'll never know the meaning of the words
                 "defeat" and "failure". . .

[*inside*]   . . . but give you something easy like
                 "cat" or "doggie" and you can't be beat!

Halloween is a sort of "anything goes" fun time. Cards can vary from simple *wishes—*

[*outside*]   KNOCK! KNOCK!
                 Who's there?
                 SHERWOOD!
                 Sherwood who?

[*inside*]   Sherwood like to wish you a
                 Happy Halloween!

—to warm and *romantic—*

[*outside*]   Don't know if I'm a trick or a treat

[*inside*]   . . . but I'm all yours!

—to just plain silly:

[*outside*]   It's Halloween, and to ward off vampires
                 wear this around your neck—

[*inside*]   [*punch-out sign with string hole*]
                 VAMPIRES BEWARE!
                 The wearer has consumed large quantities
                 of Halloween treats—This blood may
                 promote fang decay!
                 HAPPY HALLOWEEN!

Halloween themes include *trick or treat, witches, ghosts, goblins,* etc.; *thinking of you, miss you, compliments, mild slams, drinking gags, suggestive humor, jokes,* and *celebrate.*

Thanksgiving is a very small studio and humorous line. Themes are mainly *compliments,* such as:

[*outside*]   [*cutish neuter pilgrim character*]
                 On Thanksgiving. . .

[*inside*]   . . . I'm thinking thankful thoughts of thee!

Other Thanksgiving themes include *wishes, celebrate, turkey, football, pilgrims, thinking of you, jokes,* and *mild slams,* usually based on the word "turkey."

Christmas is a much bigger studio and humorous season in which most everyday themes are used along with, or in combinations with, *Santa Claus, reindeer, mistletoe, snowmen,* and other traditional Christmas symbols. *Jokes* and *topical gags* are common, such as in this example:

[*outside*]   Remember the three phrases that sum up
                 the spirit of Christmas—
                 "Peace on Earth". . .
                 "Good Will to All Men". . .

[*inside*]   . . . and "Batteries Not Included"!
                 MERRY CHRISTMAS!

Mild slams can be used in places:

[*outside*]   To help him find out who's been bad,
                 Santa has many secret helpers scattered
                 about.

[*inside*]   . . . fortunately for you, some of them
                 can be bribed!
                 MERRY CHRISTMAS!

And, as always, *compliments* are much in order:

[*outside*]   Christmas used to come only one day a
                 year . . .

[*inside*]   . . . then I met you!
                    MERRY CHRISTMAS!

New Year's is traditionally a time for *drinking gags, celebrate, jokes,* and *resolutions,* but it is equally, even if less obviously, a time for *wishes, compliments,* and *thinking of you.*

There you have them, most of the basic captions and themes used in studio and humorous cards. Of course there will be others that one company or another will use, and there are many in this chapter that several companies will not want. It's really up to you as a writer to find out how the needs of each company stack up. And there are two ways of doing this. First, get out into the card stores and learn. There's no better way to find out what a company wants than to see what it produces. The card shops, the drugstores, the department stores, discount chains, groceries—wherever the cards are, that's where you should go.

Once you have a pretty good idea of what a company produces, you can go to the editor with more specific questions. Some editors publish needs lists, and even those who don't are generally receptive to serious inquiries about their current needs. Editors rarely have time for long, detailed communications, but most are happy to keep their writers informed. After all, informed writers don't tend to waste an editor's valuable time with submissions that are nowhere near what the editor wants. On the contrary, the submissions are usually very close to what the editor is looking for—close enough, we hope, to eventually bring that informed writer a thank you and a well-deserved check.

Where to Get Funny Ideas

by Larry Sandman

As a studio and humorous greeting card editor, I'm often asked the question, "Where can I go to get funny ideas?" I like to recommend bathroom walls, but for some reason, people never seem to be satisfied with that response, so, as a second resort, I suggest "everyday life." It doesn't sound very romantic, I'll admit—nothing like if I'd said, "There's this little sidewalk cafe by the Seine, on the outskirts of Paris. Go there after the second spring rain, sit at the third table, order the house coffee, sip it slowly, and when you're done, look on the bottom of your saucer . . . your funny ideas will be written there." But then, life can't be all romance.

Now, where were we before I tripped and fell into the Seine? Oh yes—we were looking for funny ideas in everyday life. What it lacks in romance, life makes up for in humor. I think that's chiseled on a rock somewhere. It only stands to reason then that in our search for funny ideas, we should go to the things that make up our everyday lives—our books, our television, our music, our language, and our greeting cards!

Books: Many kinds of books can be helpful in our search for funny ideas: joke books, limerick books, books of nonsense verse, collections of anecdotes, one-liners, riddles; also books of skits, humorous short stories, and collections of humor from newspaper columns. Any kind of humor book can be helpful.

I once got an idea for a rather crazy studio Easter card from a book of games. One of the games involved trying to complete words that all had the sound of *egg* somewhere in them—words like *egg-cellent* and *egg-centric.* For some reason I eventually lost interest in the *egg* sound, but my mind continued to play with the idea of egg puns. The next day I went in to work, sat down with our top studio writer, and together we created:

The Egg That Saved America

An EGG-citing Easter Legend . . .

On Easter Day, 1773, the young daughter of a furniture SHELLacker named WHITE, PEELED off her clothing and LAID, FRYING in the sun on the POACH of her seaside cottage, when suddenly she noticed DOZENS of barbarian warships landing on the beach. Knowing that she'd just DYE if the barbarians saw her SETTING there in the RAW, she SCRAMBLED into the cottage. In her EGG-citement the young CHICK knocked an egg off of a table and into a bucket of paint. The bucket fell over and the egg rolled off the POACH and down to the beach where it was discovered by the HARD-BOILED barbarian captain. Intrigued by its color, the captain held the egg up and turned it OVER EASY. Suddenly it slipped through his fingers and broke open upon his face. He stood SHELL-shocked as his men CACKLED. "Ha! Ha!" they CRACKED, "Who would follow a captain with EGG ON HIS FACE?" The barbarians climbed back into their ships, battened down the HATCHes and FLEW THE COOP, never to return.

. . . and ever since that day it's been an American tradition to color eggs every Easter to commemorate one of our country's biggest BREAKS!

HAPPY EASTER!

(and that's no YOLK!)

Television and radio: These mass media are good sources for all sorts of humorous ideas, and because they do have such large audiences, chances are whatever subjects you glean from the airwaves will have widespread recognition—a positive factor when it comes to selling your cards. Radio DJs use a lot of humor in their continuity between songs, some of which can from time to time be adaptable to greeting cards. Television situation comedies and talk shows are always potential sources, as are commercials. Here are two ideas that came from radio and TV advertisements. The first is a natural response to the banking and savings and loan institution practice of giving premium gifts to savers who make deposits of a certain size:

[*outside*]   HAPPY BIRTHDAY!
                  You can have any of
                     these gifts FREE!!!
                  [*picture of luggage, radio, blender, etc.*]

[*inside*]   Just deposit $1000 or more
                  in my savings account.

The second example came into my mind when I saw an advertisement for MasterCard on television. It struck me at the time that the word *credit* as used in *credit card* could be taken in two different ways. Opting for the noncommercial connotation, I worked up this general Mother's Day card idea:

[*page 1*]   [*pleasant character to represent mother*]
                  Especially for You
                  It's Mother's Day, and time you got
                     the credit that you're due . . .

[*page 2*]   So here's a special "credit card"
                  especially made for you!

[*page 3*]   [*credit card with perforated border so it can be
                            punched out*]
                  Mother's Day Credit Card
                  Issued to
                  Who deserves special credit for always being
                  thoughtful, generous, loving and caring.
                  Signed
                  Date
                  HAVE A WONDERFUL MOTHER'S
                                  DAY!

Magazines and newspapers: Daily papers, tabloids, magazines, and journals can spark ideas. Comics; humor magazines like *Mad, Cracked,* and *The National Lampoon;* cartoon, joke, and game periodicals can all be sources of adaptations. *Reader's Digest* has a lot of jokes and anecdotes. Music, fashion, and gossip magazines can be the sources of trendy ideas. And don't forget *Time, Newsweek,* or *U.S. News and World Report* for topical ideas. And, of course, there are always the advertisements. A headache relief medicine advertisement in a women's magazine got me thinking about all of the aches and pains that led to this general get well card:

[*page 1*]   HEARD YOU'VE GOT:
___ A NASTY COLD
___ A NASTY HOT
___ A TUMMY ACHE
___ THE BLAHS
___ A NASTY THIRST
___ FRED'S FUNGUS
___ HOOF AND MOUTH DISEASE
___ MULTIPLE OUCHIES
___ A NASTY MIND
___ PLUMBING PROBLEMS
___ THE YOU-KNOW-WHATS
___ OTHER

[*page 3*]   HOPE YOU:
___ BOUNCE FORWARD
___ BOUNCE BACK
___ ENJOY SOAP OPERAS
___ EAT YOUR CHICKEN SOUP
___ STAY DOWN WIND
___ DON'T GIVE IT TO ME
___ HAVE MEDICAL INSURANCE
___ HAVE ROOM IN YOUR BED
___ SOBER UP

_____ HAVE ME IN YOUR WILL
_____ GET NURSE KREMPS
_____ OTHER
GET WELL SOON!

Music: Song titles or well-known lines from songs can be a source of humorous ideas. Some lines, such as, "If I said you have a beautiful body, would you hold it against me?" come made to order. Or a line can be adapted and changed to a sentiment like, "If I asked you to hop in the tub with me, would it get me in hot water?" Parodies of well-known songs are possibilities, too. Pop songs and standards are the most obvious places to look for ideas. Children's songs and nursery rhymes are also worth looking into. Here's a studio Baby Congrats card that sprung from a well-known children's song:

[*page 1*]   *CONGRATULATIONS!*
                and to the new star at your house . . .

[*page 3*]   Tinkle, tinkle, little star!

Quotations, proverbs and clichés: Popular usages of the English language are an outstanding source of humorous ideas. Slogans, well-known expressions—some from way back, some very up to date—might be exploited. Here are examples of card ideas using each of these three sources:

[*page 1*]   "A thing of beauty
                is a joy forever."
                —Keats

[*page 3*]   Happy Birthday,
                you beautiful thing!

[*page 1*]   It's your birthday, so remember . . .
                Don't put off till tomorrow what you can do
                today . . .

[*page 3*]   'cause if you like it today,
              you can do it again tomorrow!
              HAPPY BIRTHDAY!

[*page 1*]   You're 29, Dearie?
              I'll buy that!

[*page 3*]   . . . I'll buy anything that's been reduced!
              HAPPY BIRTHDAY!

Greeting cards: There's probably no easier-to-adapt source of greeting card ideas than other greeting cards that have already been published. And oftentimes, the rewritten sentiment is superior to the original. When writing from other greeting cards you have the advantage of having all the necessary parts already there— the cute, clever, or funny gag and the me-to-you message that is usually lacking in raw materials picked up from TV, magazines, or elsewhere.

Of course when you're rewriting cards, it's essential that you change more than just a couple of words. It is essential, both legally and ethically, that you change the idea enough so that the new card is distinctly different from the one that inspired your new creation. If you have any doubt about whether or not your idea is too close to the original, hold on to it until you are more experienced and can make a better judgment. If you are experienced, but still aren't sure about your idea, it's best to leave it out. It's not worth risking your good reputation to get one sale.

There are several ways to use a published greeting card as a source of ideas for a new card. One way of using the old card is to ignore the sentiment that is on the card and try to write a new sentiment to go with the art. Or, try using only the outside of the existing card, creating a new punchline for the inside. Many lead-ins can be used for several different punchlines. In fact, some lead-ins are so universal that they have become accepted as *formulas*. There is certainly nothing wrong with using any of these *formula lead-ins* to create your own cards. Most professionals use standard lead-ins over and over.

Here are some standard formula lead-ins and examples of one way in which each lead-in was finished off:

Lead-in: Birthdays are like . . .
      Birthdays are like beers . . .
      The more you have, the easier it is to lose count!

Lead-in: For your birthday, I'm getting you a bottle of . . .
      For your birthday, I'm getting you a bottle of OLD UNDERSHORTS . . .
      One drink and you're on your behind!

Lead-in: Happy Birthday, and may your . . . . never . . . .
      Happy Birthday, and may your swash never buckle!

Lead-in: Some good news and some bad news about your . . .
      Some good news and some bad news about your condition . . .
      The bad news is that your X rays were accidentally sent to a local veterinarian.
      Now for the good news . . .
      . . . you'll be back on all fours in no time!

Lead-in: We were made for each other . . .
      We were made for each other . . .
      I've got a screw loose and you're a nut!

There are many more lead-ins that can be used over and over

like this, and new ones are being created all the time. In fact, it is within the realm of possibility that you, yourself might invent a lead-in that will someday be picked up and used by other writers. The best way to become familiar with formula lead-ins is to spend a lot of time at the card counter reading and studying different leads. It's also a good idea to find out if your editors have any formulas that they don't need. Sometimes an editor will have all of the "Birthdays are like" cards that he can use. If that's the case, there's no sense sending him yours, because even if he really likes them, he probably won't buy them.

There is more information on how to "bounce off" published cards in the next chapter, which gets into specific formulas for studio and humorous writing.

All in all, there are many sources of humorous ideas. There are books, television and radio, magazines and newspapers, music, quotations, proverbs, clichés, and published greeting cards. And in the next chapter we'll get into how to write ideas from scratch, without references. If after that you feel the need to come back to me with the question, "Where can I go to get funny ideas?"—well, there's still the bathroom walls . . .

How to Write Humor While in Solitary Confinement

by Larry Sandman

In previous chapters we've been introduced to studio and humorous greeting cards, and we've learned what to be funny about and where to find ideas. In this chapter we're going to deal with how to pull ideas out of your head. Working on the premise that you can write humor without references, provided you have some knowledge as to how to get at those locked-up ideas, we're going to put our theory to the test—by giving you the *formulas* for creating humor, then turning you loose to see what you can do. If this chapter works the way I hope it will, you'll be able to write humor with virtually no references and no outside help. I'm not expecting either one of us to ever be shut off from the outside world, but isn't it a comforting thought to know that all you will need to amuse yourself (should the situation arise) are your humor formulas, a pointed stick, and a dusty floor?

In this chapter we are going to deal with the following humor formulas: *exaggeration, understatement, literal interpretation, reverse, misdirection, repetition, substitution, wordplay, parody,* and *zany.* We are also going to look at a few special *formats* in studio cards: *shaggy dog tales, checklists, question and answer cards, sight gags, attachment cards,* and *die-cut cards,* with the purpose of showing how you can get ideas by writing for a particular format.

Exaggeration: The most common of all humor formulas, exaggeration, is just what the name suggests, the taking of some aspect of a situation and blowing it out of proportion to the point where it becomes funny. Here's a good example of the exaggeration formula on a birthday card:

[*page 1*]   Don't let your age worry you . . .
              you're not old . . .

[*page 3*]   I've got unpaid bills older than you!

In this card, both the receiver's youthfulness and the age of the unpaid bills are exaggerated. Exaggeration can be used for virtually any caption. For an illness card, you might start out, "I know a guy who was sooo sick . . ."

Understatement: Understatement is the opposite of exaggeration. It is saying much less than you really mean. Here's a Miss You card based on understatement:

[*page 1*]   I'm lonesome . . .

[*page 3*]   . . . any suggestions?

This card is so low-keyed that it stands out, which is the very purpose of understatement—to draw a lot of attention by making too *little* noise. Here's an Our Anniversary card that uses understatement in much the same way:

[*page 1*]   It's Our Anniversary, and if you and I aren't careful . . .

[*page 3*]   . . . this could develop into something serious!

Literal interpretation: This formula is based on taking a major word in the message very literally where it wouldn't regularly be expected to be taken that way. Sometimes it is a word with a double meaning, as in the following example:

[*page 1*]   [*donkey in party hat, wildly celebrating*]
                Know what this is???

[*page 3*]   . . . another silly ass birthday card!

Again the key word has a double meaning in this example:

[*page 1*]   I really racked my brain finding
                just the right birthday greeting for you . . .

[*page 3*]   . . . actually, what happened was I caught
                my head in the damn card rack!

There's no double meaning in this third example, but the humor is derived from a very literal interpretation of the words "sweet and sugary":

| [*page 1*] | Since it's your birthday, hope you don't mind a card that says something sweet and sugary . . . |

| [*page 3*] | . . . MAPLE SYRUP! |

Reverse: This formula reverses the normal or expected roles of things, as in this Belated Birthday card:

| [*page 1*] | [*animated rock*] Don't know why I forgot your birthday . . |

| [*page 3*] | . . . I must have had humans in my head! |

Misdirection: This formula is based on leading the reader to expect one thing and then giving him something else. It is one of the funnier types of formulas, as these Birthday cards will show:

| [*page 1*] | I heard if I gave you a thousand dollars for your birthday you'd like nothing better . . . |

| [*page 3*] | . . . so here's nothing (hope you like it better) |

| [*page 1*] | For your birthday I put $2 on a long shot at Hialeah that started at 25 to 1 |

| [*page 3*] | Unfortunately, the other horses started at 12:30. |

Repetition: In this formula the humor is based on repeating a word or words from the setup in the punchline. In the following example, almost all of the setup is repeated:

| [*page 1*] | You're not just another pretty face . . . |

[*page 3*]   You're another pretty face that's having
                  another Birthday!

Substitution: The act of replacing an expected word with another gives this formula its name. In the following Birthday card,
the key word in the punchline is replaced with a similar sound
which has a totally different meaning:

[*page 1*]   What rhymes with Hex, starts with an "S,"
                  and is needed often by people our age?

[*page 3*]   SPECS!

Wordplay: This is one of the major humor formulas for use in
greeting cards. It includes any kind of play with words, puns, playing with sounds, and taking words apart and putting them back
together again. Here is a simple but effective use of a pun:

[*page 1*]   [*wooly mammoth*]
                  Happy Birthday!

[*page 3*]   HAVE A MAMMOTH CELEBRATION!

The following birthday card plays with word sounds:

[*page 1*]   It's your Birthday, so be happy!
                  You're not a youngster!
                  You're not an oldster!

[*page 3*]   You're not a hamster, either!

This last wordplay, coming up, derives its humor from breaking a
word apart to create two new words with connotations far different
from those of the original word:

[*page 1*]   Have a Happy Birthday . . .

[*page 3*]   And may your swash never buckle!

Parody: The takeoffs of serious works are the basis for the parody
formula. Here's an example of a card that parodies romantic prose

cards. It also borrows from the exaggeration formula to help make the parody sillier:

[*page 1*]   Our relationship will last
                    till the stars fall from the sky . . .
                    till the mountains wash to sea . . .
                    till the sun spins out of its orbit . . .

[*page 3*]   . . . till we drive each other nuts!

Zany: This is the kind of humor that is often described as "off the wall." It's wild, undisciplined, unfounded, and often hilariously funny. Here's a General Friendship card that meets all the requirements for being zany:

[*page 1*]   [*in formal lettering:*]
                    Special Warning from the
                    Nuclear Safety Administration

                    IN EXACTLY TEN SECONDS
                    YOUR UNDERWEAR
                    WILL BURST INTO FLAMES!

[*page 3*]   You may laugh now, but you're going
                    to look silly in six seconds!

Those are the humorous formulas. By taking an appropriate greeting-card-sending situation, such as a birthday, then by applying one of these formulas to some aspect of the sending situation—either an aspect of the card receiver, or of the situation itself—you should be able to create humorous ideas that can be used for studio or humorous cards.

Don't expect immediate phenomenal success. It takes time to get a firm grasp on the different formulas and how they can be used. But with time it will come, and your ability to create humorous ideas from scratch will improve. That's assuming that you work with the materials presented here, and assuming also that you came into this with a sense of humor and at least a small amount of creativity. No tools are any better than the workman who is handling them.

Before leaving this chapter I'd like to share a few special *formats* with you. These formats apply basically to studio cards, though all studio cards tend to spill over at least a little bit into humorous cards. These are groupings of cards by a general editorial or design style, or by some outstanding aspect that all of the cards in a particular grouping have in common. Though, as groupings, they are lost somewhere between themes and oblivion, they are significant groups, and, in fact, any one of these formats might be requested by an editor at some time.

Shaggy dog tales: These are rather long, drawn out, usually ridiculous tales that are designed to build to a climax. They usually end with a rather elaborate pun, that being the punchline toward which the entire story builds. Here's an example:

[*page 1*]   Once upon a time there was a king named Ed who reigned over a small country in Southern Utah. He was a good and wise king, but he had one very bad habit . . . King Ed just loved animals, and he kept bringing them to live in the castle with him . . .

[*page 2*]   He had deer and water buffalo and foxes . . . all sorts of game in every room of the castle. The people for the kingdom finally got fed up with this stinky situation, and decided he must be dethroned, and all the game returned to their natural habitat.

[*page 3*]   Thus ended the reign of Good King Ed! But it was a very monumental time in history! It was the first time . . .

[on flap covering punchline]
Here goes
[under flap]
. . . that the "reign was called on account of
game"

Shaggy dog tales are most commonly used in General Birthday, Belated Birthday, and General Friendship captions. They are a glaring exception to most studio card rules, being too long by regular standards, and often with no readily recognizable sending purpose. You will still have your best chance of selling an unsolicited shaggy dog tale if it is applicable to a normal greeting card sending situation. Most shaggy dogs are written backwards, starting with the punchline, then going back and writing the accompanying tale.

Checklist: This is the kind of card that gives the sender a bunch of choices as to what he wants to say, by presenting the choices on a list. Here's a checklist written for a Birthday, from Both card:

[page 1]   *From Both of Us.*
Dear: — Friend
— Relative
— Neighbor
— Special Person
— Other
We knew it had to be your BIRTHDAY
from:
— The smell of burning wax
— The sold-out sign at the liquor
store
— The screams of distress
— The screams of delight
— The screams of police sirens
— Other

[page 3]   So we rushed right out and got you this card
to say:

— Birthdays happen to the best of us
— Have a helluva good time
— Call if you need help raising bail
— Take that lampshade off your head, you look ridiculous
— Hope your day's as nice as you
— Many happy returns
— Other

Checklists should be as widely sendable as possible, with a good variety of messages, ranging from warm compliments to mild slams.

Question and answer: These are cards that feature answers to questions on a greeting-card related theme. The questions and answers should be funny or clever, usually about eight on a card. Here's an example of a question-and-answer-type card:

[*page 1*]   *For Your Birthday*
Auntie Betts answers your questions about getting older!

[*page 3*]   [*questions printed on top of flaps, answers underneath*]

HOW CAN
I AVOID
GETTING
GRAY
AROUND
THE TEM-
PLES?
Stay away
from tem-
ples.

WHAT
CAN I DO
ABOUT
PEOPLE
WHO
MAKE
BAD
JOKES
ABOUT
MY AGE?
Hit 'em
with your
cane.

HOW CAN
I LIVE TO
BE 100?
Live it up
till you're
99, then be
very careful.

HOW CAN
I AVOID
WRINKLES?
Use only
permanent
press.

DO PEO-
PLE WHO
AVOID
SEX AND
DRINKING
LIVE
LONGER?
No, it just
seems
longer.

HOW CAN
I MAKE
MYSELF
LOOK
YOUNGER?
Hang
around with
older peo-
ple.

HOW CAN
I AVOID
FALLEN
ARCHES?
Stay away
from decay-
ing build-
ings.

HOW
WILL I
KNOW
WHEN I'M
OLD?
When you
and your
teeth start
sleeping in
different
rooms.

Sight gags: These are cards in which the entire message, except perhaps for a caption and tag, are carried by the artwork. Sight gags can amount to only a single page 1 design, or they can include a series of cartoonlike progressions. One clever sight gag features a neuter character who is standing alone in the first of five panels. In the second panel, a dumptruck backs up and begins dumping its load at the neuter's feet. In the third and fourth panels the truck continues to empty its load, which is a quivering mass that is apparently emitting such sounds as *Ha's, Ho's,* and *Hee's.* In the fifth and final panel the truck is pulling away and the sentiment tag reads "Wishing you a load of laughs on your birthday!"

A much simpler idea is a card with nothing on the front except an artist's rendering of a toilet plunger. Inside is the message, "Thinking of your kisses . . ."

If you draw well and have a good visual imagination you might want to try some sight gags. If you don't draw, brief written descriptions will do for simple ones, like the plunger idea. It's extremely difficult to sell more complicated sight gags without at least a rough sketch of how the art would look.

Attachment cards: These are the cards that have some sort of small object either glued or taped to them, and an appropriate message that ties in with the attachment. One of the most common attachments found on cards today is a mirror, usually made of thin foil, tightly adhered to the inside of the card. A number of good sentiments have been written for mirror attachment cards, such as this funny Birthday message:

[*page 1*] *Have a Good Time on Your Birthday*
but remember, experts say that years
and years of overindulgence in drinking
and sex can ultimately lead to complete
physical dissipation . . .
Just look what it did to THIS poor devil . . .

[*page 3*] [*mirror*]
HAPPY BIRTHDAY!

It's a good idea to ask your editor if he is buying attachment ideas before you submit them. Many companies are not using attachments, and sending them in is a waste of time and postage.

Die-cut cards: We've already discussed die-cut cards in the hu-

morous chapter, but die-cuts are often used in studio cards, too. In
fact a die-cut can be an essential part of the humor in a studio card.
Here are a couple of examples of studio cards whose sentiments are
written, calling for special die-cuts:

[*page 1*]   Didn't want to cut any corners when
                    I went shopping for your Birthday present!

[*page 3*]   [*upper right corner cut off*]
                    Well, just one.
                    HAPPY BIRTHDAY!

[*page 1*]   Here's a special *tongue twister*
                    for your birthday!

[*page 3*]   [*die-cut slit large enough to stick tongue into*]
                    Stick tongue through here
                    and turn upside down
                    HAPPY BIRTHDAY!

Die-cuts, when cleverly done, add a lot of value to a studio or
humorous card, and since it's a relatively inexpensive operation,
it's one that most companies like to use.

All of the formats mentioned in this chapter are rather specific
types of cards which will be done by some companies and not by
others. Editors' needs will vary, too, from time to time, so you can
save yourself a lot of time and trouble by checking in with your
editors to find out what they need. Don't be bashful. Every editor
that *I* know would rather say, "Sure, I'm interested in attachment
cards," or "No, thanks—we're not in the market," than to have to
wade through envelopes of submissions in which every other card
is something his company doesn't even buy.

Creating and Selling Promotions

by Richard E. Myles

In greeting cards, promotions are a group of designs with a central theme, both visual and verbal. Promotions can be based on almost any type of greeting card. They can be conventional in thought and feeling, with all of the cards sharing a common design theme, such as watercolor florals. They can be humorous, featuring photographs of fruits and vegetables with silly messages like "Orange you glad it's your birthday?" or "How you bean?" They can be informal, with cute characters and simple, pleasant sentiments like "Know who's nicer 'n you? Nobody—that's who!" They can be inspirational, with beautiful verses lettered over nature photographs. Or they can be romantic personal relationship cards with soft-focus photos and affectionate short prose sentiments.

Promotions have a multiple purpose: to introduce new styling, new ideas, new characters, new formats, and to bring in *plus business.* Plus business is business over and above what would normally be expected in a greeting card department. It is business created in two ways: first, by impulse sales, and second, by increased repeat business.

Many greeting card purchases are impulse sales, those unplanned purchases that we customers make when we see a card that we simply *"have* to send to ol' what's his name." Displays of eye-catching promotions are designed to entice us into making such purchases. They're also designed to be something *different,* something unique that keeps us coming back to the same store where we can always find a card that says what we want to say in a fresh, new way.

Frankly, for the greeting card freelance writer, creating promotions can be difficult. Companies issue promotions in groups of twelve designs or more (usually more). That means getting a dozen or more sentiments accepted at one time. However, don't despair—it has been and is being done.

In addition to being a unique concept with impulse-buying appeal, a promotion theme should also be *open-ended*. This means that whatever the theme of your concept, there should be a relatively unlimited number of ideas that could be developed from it.

Another avenue is writing to existing characters or themes. Character merchandising has become an important part of every major company's offering. These are characters that were created for and first appeared on greeting cards. The best known and most successful of these is American Greetings' "Holly Hobbie." They've more recently introduced "Strawberry Shortcake." Some others include Rust Craft Greeting Cards' "Barney," Gibson Greeting Cards' "Little Friends," and Norcross's "Wishbone."

From a "Barney" card, with the dog fishing a big bone from a trash can, the sentiment reads:

[*outside*]   It's really a treat . . .

[*inside*]   . . . having you for a friend!

And here's a "Wishbone" card showing the turkey wearing an old aviator's cap:

[*outside*]   It's me!!
                   The turkey of pleasure
                   here to wish you a very happy
                   birthday!! . . .

[*inside*]   . . . the bluebird of happiness
                   couldn't make it!
                   HAPPY BIRTHDAY

Greeting cards, like comic strips and animated movie cartoons, often humanize animals. A further example of this is from Gibson's "Delightfuls," where a humorous frog appears on the cover with the sentiment:

[*outside*]   My love for you grows . . .

[*inside*]   . . . by leaps and bounds!

A promotion can direct itself to an editorial theme, such as love, inspiration, nostalgia, and the like. Rust Craft combines themes in its "The Wonders of Nature." One card with a photograph of a sunset reads:

[*outside*]   Friendship is the evening star
                    that strengthens with the setting sun.

[*inside*]   Our friendship means more to me each day!

And, from Gibson Greeting Cards' "Moments to Remember," a card with a basket of roses on the cover says:

[*outside*]   *For Someone Special*

[*inside*]   Some people seem to walk through life
                    with a smile and a gentle word
                    for everyone . . .
                    and everywhere they go they leave
                    a little warmth, a little love.
                    You are one of those special people

American Greetings continues to produce its highly successful "Soft Touch" line. Introduced in 1970, the visual and editorial remain in the same key. Here's an example of a Soft Touch card with a soft floral photograph on the cover and a sentiment that reads:

[*outside*]   As the years pass by,
                    some things never change . . .

[*inside*]   like my love for you . . .
                    Have a beautiful day!

Norcross has its "Gentle World" series that includes a number of promotions such as "Wags and Whiskers" and "Best Friends."

One of Hallmark Cards' many successful promotions is a series of "label cards." These are cards that feature labels from well-known products such as Campbell's Soup. The success of these cards has been due in part to everyone's familiarity with the products, especially advertisements for the products. If you can key your promotion concepts to characters, objects, or ideas that are universally known, you have a much better chance of making a sale.

A promotion can be based on a concept totally new to the greeting card field, or it can be built around old concepts presented in a new way. For example, large greeting cards were not new to the industry when, a few years ago, Barker Greeting Cards (now a division of Rust Craft) came out with a promotion of gigantic greeting cards that measured 3x5 feet when fully opened. The designs usually featured a large animal standing next to a small animal, such as a tiger and a mouse. One of the captions read, "I LUV YOU SOMETHIN' FIERCE!" These were, and continue to be, highly successful cards.

It is extremely difficult to sit down and create a promotion, and I wouldn't advise that you approach them in that way. What you should do is keep the idea of promotions in mind as you are writing other greeting cards. If you come across a concept or theme for which you are able to write several ideas, see if you can't come up with enough ideas to make it worth offering to a company as a promotion. Keep in mind that promotions generally consist of only *birthday, friendship,* and *illness* titles, and sometimes *only friendship.*

It certainly couldn't hurt to get out and see what kinds of promotions each company is selling before embarking on your own. It will give you a better idea of what kinds of sentiments a company might accept. One thing you're likely to find is that many companies allow a greater deal of freedom for writers in their promotions than in their counter lines. Ideas like the following might be suitable for promotions even though they aren't likely to appear in counter cards:

[*art: photo of suit of armor*]

[*message*]   . . . that was *some* night
                 wasn't it? . . .

or:

[*art: photo of dog peeking out from inside a toilet*]

[*message*]   Looks like it's going to be
                 another one of those days . . .

Try to send twelve to twenty-four ideas in a promotion package. Include a letter telling the editor that you are offering them as a promotion. Also explain whether or not you are willing to sell your ideas individually. Sometimes an editor does not wish to buy your promotion, but is interested in one or more of the individual card ideas. It is up to you to decide whether you would like to sell the ideas and replace them in your promotion, or whether you would rather keep the promotion intact.

Expand on your theme or concept if necessary, especially if you feel that more ideas are possible from your premise. If your promotion requires that the cards (or other products) be specially cut or folded, then try to hand cut or fold a few dummies so that the editor can see what has to be done. That allows the editor to make a better judgment about your promotion's costs and its potential worth.

If the ideas require special drawings or photographs, do the best you can to simulate a finished card, even if you're not an artist or photographer. Even the most basic drawing is usually more explanatory than no drawing at all.

Payment for promotions is usually based on the concept itself plus so many dollars for each idea you develop. In addition, if the editor decides to expand the promotion later, it's possible that he or she will come back to you for more ideas. No greeting card company has set fees for promotions. Each negotiates with the writer after viewing the promotion. Sometimes editors will just buy the concept and not the individual sentiments. If an editor is interested in a promotion he may hold it longer than conventional greeting card submissions, as it is likely that the concept will have to be reviewed by many people within the company.

One last thought about promotions: *Always keep in mind the possibilities that spring from current news events, fads, and such that are likely to have at least six months' life.* Some card companies have the ability to get cards printed and distributed extremely fast, and they are able to take advantage of events like this.

During a recent gasoline shortage, Rust Craft had a promotion called "Gas Lines." One card read:

[*outside*]   On your birthday
               do your part to help
               during the gas crisis!!!

[*inside*]   . . . Drink! don't drive . . .
               (and have a happy day!)

However, as the gas lines disappeared, so did the reason for any follow-up to this promotion. So be sure to get timely promotion ideas in quickly!

Remember, *current events* with a long enough life span to them, *new concepts* not used before in the greeting card field, *old concepts* dressed up in a new way—unique, eye-catching, impulse-sale-creating items that bring in *plus business* for greeting card companies and their customers—that's what *PROMOTIONS* are all about!

Getting
Your Ideas Ready
for Sale

Now that you have your ideas written, and they're fresh and original and timely and all the things they should be, it's simply a matter of tossing them into an envelope and bundling them off to some eagerly awaiting editor. Right? Wrong!

Just as you don't simply "dash off" some writing on a piece of paper, neither do you simply "send it off" in the mail. The way you prepare and submit your ideas is as important as the writing itself, because it can mean the difference between rejection and sales. So let's get busy and learn the things we have to know about *marketing* our ideas.

One of the first things to consider is the idea itself. *Is it ready for market?* Here is a list of some things to watch for (the checklist includes items you would check for only in specific types of cards, such as studio or conventional; so use each item accordingly):

1. *Does the idea have a me-to-you message?* This is the basic ingredient in any greeting card. It gives the reason for sending the card: because you want to say something to the person you are sending the card to. You might say it formally, sentimentally, amusingly, informally, or hilariously; but however you say it, the me-to-you message is the reason you or anyone else sends greeting cards.

It is possible to get away occasionally with a joke gag that doesn't have a me-to-you message in a studio card, but it is a rare bird even there and best avoided until your feet are not only wet, but soaked.

2. *Is the idea relevant to the occasion?* This means, is the subject matter in your idea normally associated with the occasion? For example, cake for birthdays, thermometer for get wells, celebrating for anniversaries, Santa Claus for Christmas, and like so. Here are some subjects that are *not* relevant to the occasion: drinking for Halloween or Easter, trick or treat for birthdays, gifts for Thanksgiving, risque gags for Bar Mitzvah, and so on. The more relevant your idea is to the occasion, the better are your chances of selling it.

3. *Does your idea use a phony situation?* Here is an example of one:

When you chased your nurse around your bed last night, it proved one thing . . .
. . . you've taken a turn for the nurse!

Obviously, the patient did not chase the nurse around the bed—unless the patient was a male editor, because you know how they are—so this is an attempt to set up a phony situation in order to get to a punchline. When the gag is a good one, and you resort to a phony situation, it simply means you haven't worked the idea out properly. Put it aside for awhile and then try it again later, but don't send it out until it's right and logical within its premises.

4. *Is the idea generally sendable? Who will send it? To whom?* Many ideas submitted for cards are good gags but just aren't usable as greeting cards. For example:

A bachelor is a man who doesn't have to wash a dish . . .
. . . until he wants to eat from one!

Now this might be useful as an epigram in a magazine, but it's no greeting card. And to those of you who say you could send this idea to a bachelor friend, I'll agree with you, you could, but why would you?

Or as another example, the idea might be one that has to be sent to a man by a woman, but it is too risque for a woman ever to buy it. So although a lot of male editors might fall off their editorial chairs laughing, they won't pay you a cent for your gag and all you've managed to do is bring a little sunlight into their bleak lives, which might gain you a few lifelong friends but won't put any money in your pocket.

Check your idea carefully and make certain it is as generally sendable as you can make it. One good check is to try to think of a couple of people you know who could send the card or who could receive it. Would *you* send the card? Could it be sent *to* you? By whom?

Another thing that will make the idea more generally sendable is to keep the personal pronoun *I* out of it. Remember, there are many cases where two or more people send a single card. If a lot of your ideas have an *I* in them, try to write it out. Your material will be improved. Here is how it might work:

I don't want you to think of this as just a birthday card . . .
. . . I want you to think of it as a present!

Don't think of this as just a birthday card . . .
. . . think of it as a present!

Notice that when you leave the *I* out, the idea shortens, and remember that old saying, "Brevity rhymes with levity!" Which brings us to our next item.

5. *Is your idea as brief as possible?* This doesn't mean that your idea should be short simply for the sake of being short. There are times when you may even have to lengthen a buildup to make the punchline more effective. What it does mean is that your idea should contain no useless words, words that do not contribute to the idea. Any extra words distract the reader's attention from the meat of your idea. Cut the useless words out! For example, instead of saying something like:

Sixty cents is a lot more money than I ordinarily spend for a birthday card . . .
. . . but all of the sixty-cent presents looked cheap!

say:

Ordinarily I don't spend sixty cents for a birthday card . . .
. . . but the sixty-cent presents looked cheap!

6. *Is your idea written in plain, simple language?* When writing your ideas, use ordinary, everyday language—words that average people can understand. Don't say things like *"don't be disagreeably effusive";* say *"don't shoot your mouth off";* and not *"terribly disheveled,"* but *"messy."* Greeting cards are no place to try to be flowery or show how many big words you know . . . or to try to play "Stump the Editor." Because if you *do* stump him, he won't reach

for his dictionary, he'll reach for a rejection slip.

7. *Is the idea funny?* It'd be nice if there were some simple rule to help you decide whether or not your idea is actually funny. But there isn't. And there never will be—at least not until we all start laughing at the same things. As long as one man's joke is another man's pun, it will be difficult, and at times downright impossible, to determine what is funny. The only things that will help you tell to some degree whether or not an idea is funny is experience.

Fortunately you don't have to wait for experience to come to you. It's available all around you in the form of greeting cards, joke books, humorous stories, comedians, television, anything and everything that contains humor. By burying yourself in all the various types of humor available to you today, you gain the benefit of the judgment of all the editors, writers, and performers responsible for the publication and showing of humorous material. Soon you will find yourself able to tell fairly well what is *amusing,* what is *funny,* and what is *hilarious.* The more humor you read and study, the more experience you will gain, and you'll soon learn to judge your own material well enough to tell whether it is as funny and punchy as it could be, or whether it needs more work. Read and listen to all the humor you can find. It's the quickest way to gain experience.

8. *Is the humor understandable?* Humor that isn't understandable can be the result of several things. It could be too subtle—the general public just isn't that sharp when it comes to humor. That's why your most popular comedians are the ones who hit you in the face with their humor. You don't have to try to figure it out—they spell it all out and let you have it wide open with no guesswork. Don't try to be subtle or cute with your humor. Make it obvious. Club 'em over the head with it!

Another thing that can kill greeting card humor is the use of little-known or old happenings, expressions, sayings, songs, historical events, and so on, that the writer assumes everyone knows because he and his friends do. Don't work gags around old expressions or little-known events or whathaveyou's that aren't current. Use things that are in the news and popular now.

A third killer of greeting card humor is the local or "in" joke. Basing a joke on something that is well known in Los Angeles or in New York may get you a lot of laughs in Los Angeles or in New York, but it isn't going to sell greeting cards in Burlington, Vermont. The same goes for jokes that are only funny if you belong to the Elks or the Knights of Columbus, or if you hang around the men's locker room at the Loyal Order of Sports. These may get great laughs among your friends, but don't try them on greeting cards because no one will understand them, and the editor will just send you a rejection slip that is very easy to understand.

What this all means is that to be funny, humor—any kind of humor—must be about things that people will recognize. It's as simple as that.

9. *Is the occasion identified on the cover?* Although many writers may not be aware of it, greeting cards are designed perhaps more with the buyer in mind than the receiver. There is an old saying somewhere in the greeting card industry (what would an industry be without an old saying?) that the card design makes the buyer pick up the card, and the text sells the card. Now, since cards are usually bought for a specific occasion, card companies try to identify the occasion on the cover or outside of the card, so that it will be easy for the buyer to spot the kind of card he wants from among the hundreds displayed in a rack.

The occasion can be identified in two ways. Either it can be identified through design—hearts on Valentine's Day, Santa Claus and winter scenes on Christmas cards, green colors and leprechauns on St. Patrick's Day—or, since there are no identifying colors or designs that can be used for *everyday* cards, it can be done with text. For example: *Happy Birthday to a girl who. . .,* or *On your Anniversary, be sure. . .,* or *Congratulations, Graduate, looks like you've. . . .*

10. *Have you worked your idea out to its best possible form?* Many ideas that editors receive contain excellent subject matter that could be cutely illustrated or would make a slightly different and fresh-sounding greeting card, but the idea just doesn't hold together.

Now, besides the fact that you should never send an idea out until you're completely satisfied that it is in the best possible form you can put it in, another important factor is that most editors will cut the writer's pay when the idea has to be rewritten. Sometimes the cut will be almost half of the writer's regular pay.

When you're considering whether or not your idea is in its best possible form, think of the money. Nothing concentrates a writer's mind better than the thought of losing money.

11. *Are you using old, worn-out rhymes?* Watch for rhymes like *way, day, say, may, play; love, above; years, tears, fears; do, you; kiss, bliss.* They, and many like them, have been used too many times for too many years. Look for fresh, new rhymes, new ways to say old things. The extra time you spend could bring many extra dollars back in sales. Don't send rhymes out that are dull with triteness . . . find new rhymes that sparkle with brightness.

12. *Are you using the word* you? The most important word in greeting cards is *you!* The least important is *I.* If your idea has more *I*'s than *you*'s in it, edit them out! Get rid of them like they were the plague; that's about what they're worth to you. If your idea doesn't have a lot of useless *I*'s in it, but it doesn't have any *you*'s in it either, then rewrite it and stick some *you*'s in there! If you don't think editors consider the word *you* important, the next time you're reading a bunch of cards, check them specifically for *you's.*

Now that you've checked your idea out thoroughly and feel that it's definitely ready for market, you have to decide what form to send it in. There are several basic forms used.

One form is to type the idea or verse out on a 3x5-inch or 4x6-inch card as shown below:

[front of card]
Now that you're older, remember that if you neck, drink, and stay out late . . . men will call you FAST . . .
. . . just as FAST as they can get a phone!

HAPPY BIRTHDAY

[*back of card*]

(Name)   (Idea code number)

(Address)

These flat cards are a submission form that you can use for ideas for all greeting cards—conventional, inspirational, informal, juvenile, humorous, or studio.

Another form you can use for studio and humorous cards is a simple folded sheet of paper, ranging from a folded 4x6-inch sheet to actual card size. The buildup is then typed or neatly hand-lettered on the outside of the folded paper, and the punchline is put on the right inside page. For studio and humorous card ideas, this outside/inside form of presentation is much more effective than the flat card because it hides the punchline until the buildup has been read, thus insuring that the surprise ending of the gag has been retained.

There are, however, some editors who insist that you submit all your ideas on 3x5-inch cards. For them, regardless of your personal feelings or preference, you must send your ideas in the way they want them. Personally, if the pay rate was high enough, I would send ideas to them on the back of a camel, front or rear hump, if that was what it took to sell them.

The third form of submission, used basically for studio, humorous, and juvenile cards, is to make up a complete rough *dummy* that is as close to the finished card as you can make it. This includes everything called for in the finished card: actual size, rough sketch, attachment, mechanical action, unusual folds, cutouts, color, etc. This is the best form of the three for the types of cards mentioned, and is the one most used by professional freelance writers. It is also one that anyone can learn to use regardless of *original* drawing ability.

If you're interested in completely designing a greeting card or even in becoming a professional greeting card artist—a talent you can wed to your writing ability—there are hundreds of excellent books, courses, and schools for artists available today. Being able to draw enables a writer to do many *visual gags* that he cannot do if he can only write. (A visual gag is one in which most, if not all, of the humor depends upon the drawing or series of drawings used in the card—similar to captionless cartoons. Check cards on the racks for the visual gag type.)

If you only want to learn to sketch well enough to illustrate your idea, make it understandable, and perhaps enhance it somewhat, then the easiest way is to buy a bunch of cards that have characters on them that express the basic emotions like anger, shyness, love, laughter, happiness, sorrow, etc., and then learn to draw variations of these characters in various positions. For get well ideas, buy cards with hospital beds, doctors, nurses, and medical equipment illustrated on them. For Valentine ideas, cupids, bows and arrows, hearts, and so forth. Same principle for any other type of ideas. Use the same characters and basic equipment on any of the ideas you want to illustrate. Using this method, you'll soon learn to do a professional-looking job illustrating any of your ideas.

One further thing: If you don't sketch at all, and don't want or have the time to learn, don't waste your time giving a word picture of what kind of illustration you think the card should have, unless the illustration is essential to your idea.

Giving a word picture when an illustration isn't essential to your gag just wastes your time, clutters up your form, and distracts the editor's attention away from the gag itself. Better to spend your time writing more of those fifty-dollar gags you're so good at.

If the illustration is an essential part of your idea, then, of course, suggest it. For example, in this studio card idea the illustration is part of the gag:

[*Devil blowing horn, musical note coming out of horn; along with note, like on a sheet of music, are two words:*]
You're sick? . . .

. . . that's a helluva note!

Regardless of which form you use to present your ideas, don't clutter up the front of it with routine information like your name, address, and code number. Put all of this information on the back of your form where it's out of the way until the editor needs to refer to it. And don't waste time typing or writing your name over and over. For a few dollars at most stationery stores you can buy a rubber stamp with your name and address. It will save you hours of time—time you could be using to write ideas, and the sale of just one of those ideas could more than pay for the stamp. To change the old saying: *Don't be penny-wise and time-foolish!*

At this point, you've checked your ideas out thoroughly and they are all ready for submission. But not quite. There are still a lot of do's and don't's to consider before sealing your envelope.

Make certain your name, complete address, and code number are on the back of *each* form.

Be sure your envelopes are big enough to hold your ideas. For full-size dummies, invest in heavyweight manila envelopes, available at most department and stationery stores. They come in all the convenient sizes, and though they cost a little more than regular envelopes, they are well worth the price.

Above all, *don't squeeze* your ideas into an envelope. There's nothing more annoying than trying to tear open an envelope that is crammed so full you can't even get hold of a corner of it. And don't send a return envelope that is too small to put your rejected ideas into. If that sounds silly, it is! But it happens almost every day. Why do writers do it? Who knows. Either they don't bother checking the size of their return envelope, or they have the strange idea that if the editor can't get their ideas into the return envelope, he'll buy them! And they're mistaken, of course, because we usually manage to get their ideas into their too-small return envelope.

Don't use paper clips to hold your ideas together. Paper clips make marks on the cards or dummies and you have to redo them after only two or three submissions. Use rubber bands instead, and make sure the bands are large enough to hold the ideas firmly yet not cut into the paper.

Don't clip stamps to your return envelope. There has never been a time yet when every idea from a batch has been bought, so you're bound to have returns. Consequently, your return envelope is going to be used and it is going to need stamps. Use the glue on the stamps for what it was intended, to stick the stamps onto your return envelope.

It would probably pay you to invest in a postage scale. They're very inexpensive and available at most department and stationery stores. This way you'll be sure of having the right number of stamps on your envelopes so you won't be wasting money.

One question that always seems to arise is whether or not to include a letter with your submissions. It's a question that may never be settled, but here's the closest thing around to a consensus. If you have something to say that is *pertinent* to your material, or if you have a legitimate question, then by all means include a letter with your submissions.

But do *not* include a letter simply to tell the editor that you are submitting ideas to him. He can see that. Or to list the ideas you are submitting to him. He's not going to check your list. And do *not* tell him you're just beginning and you would appreciate his considering your ideas. He's being paid to consider *all* ideas, and telling him you're just beginning is likely to put a couple of strikes against you, especially if he has had a hectic day, or a couple of new writers have just accused him of everything from plagiarism to child molesting. Besides, you're doing all this study and work and practice so you won't look like a new writer, so why tell the editor you're a new writer when you look like a professional? Let your ideas speak for themselves.

Also, don't tell the editor what rights you're offering, and how much you want for your work:

First, greeting card companies buy *all rights*.

Second, editors go out of their way to pay fair prices to their writers, but their rates are normally fixed for certain types of ideas, so *all* writers get the usual rates. This is not to say that writers who sell to an editor regularly cannot get higher than normal rates. They can, and usually do. But writers who are just beginning to sell to an editor, or who sell to him only occasionally, get the normal fixed rates.

Third, unless you're a well-known writer, poet, cartoonist, or artist, it's 99½ percent against your getting royalties for a greeting card idea. If you insist on royalties when you don't deserve them, the editor will insist on sending you a rejection slip that you do deserve. Get famous first, then worry about royalties.

Finally, remember one thing: You are never wrong in *not* including a letter with your submissions, but saying anything wrong in one can kill a sale. If you're uncertain about whether or not to include a letter and what to say, perhaps the best rule of the little finger is: *When in doubt leave it out!*

Since you're in this business to make money, it makes sense to get as much for your writing as you possibly can, so, in general, send your material to the highest paying market first. Then to the next highest paying market, and so on down the list. This is for everyday material. Seasonal material has to be sent as the editors ask for it, since most editors, but not all, will look at the seasonal ideas only at certain times of the year. Ask the editor periodically what seasonal line he will be looking at next and when will he start looking.

Ordinarily, send between ten and fifteen ideas in each batch. Less than ten wastes your time and postage, and more than fifteen overwhelms the editor, who might tend to give less of a reading to each idea.

Never address your envelope directly to the company. If you do not know the name of the editor, then address your envelope to the type of editor for whom your ideas are intended: humorous editor, studio editor, conventional editor, juvenile editor, weird editor. If you do not so address your submission, then the company mailroom must open your envelope to find out where it's supposed to go and even what's in it, which could result in some of your ideas getting lost, or being cut by the electric openers most companies now use. In addition, the extra handling causes the company added expense which doesn't help your cause any.

Remember, you know how to write, you know the techniques used to write sentiment and humor, you know everything necessary to sit at your typewriter and start writing. You don't have to wait for the mood to strike you. You can sit down and write any time you want to, even when you don't want to but have to. The only mood-writers there are, are those who haven't properly learned all the techniques of writing, and are too lazy or lacking in ambition to learn them.

And if you say that's a lot of hogwash, that a true writer can only write when the so-called *muse* is with him, then you're forgetting thousands of newspaper, television, radio, industrial, greeting card, public relations, advertisement, and magazine writers and editors who write *on demand* day after day and year after year. If they can do it, so can you. Don't mistake laziness for a lack of the muse: Ain't no such animal!

Once you get your ideas out in the mail, don't sit around and wait impatiently for them to come back. You can't pray your ideas into selling. The only thing that is going to bring a constant *inflow* of checks is a constant *outflow* of ideas. Spend your time working and writing, not waiting and wishing.

If, when you get your rejects back, there is a note from the editor telling you that he has an idea similar to one of yours already in his line, don't panic. He's not accusing you of copying the idea or trying to steal it from his company. He is simply letting you know that he already has one like yours so that if you spot it on the racks six months hence you won't accuse *him* of stealing it from *you.*

What do you do about it? If he simply says that the idea is similar to one he already has, he's probably just talking about the basic premise of the gag, and so you're safe in continuing to submit it to other companies.

If, however, he says your idea is identical with, or exactly like, a card his company already has out or that he just bought from another writer, or words to that effect (he may even send you a copy of that other idea), then you would probably be better off destroying your form and not taking a chance on it.

Some writers make it a practice either to send the editor their destroyed idea or to tell him that they have destroyed it, and to thank him for letting them know about the duplication. They feel that this way it lets the editor know that they did not copy his company's card but had simply and honestly written an idea like it, which frequently happens. In general, it's probably a good practice to include such a note with your next submission to the editor. He may be curious about what you did with the idea, and he'll undoubtedly appreciate your thanking him.

Never stop submitting an idea as long as you feel it's a good one. Humor and sentiment are constantly changing things, and what was tearfully sentimental ten years ago may be corny today. The type of humor that no one thought funny last year may be considered hilarious next year. In addition, the editors may have only rejected your idea because, even though it was a good one, they had no place in their lines for it. An editor might buy a couple of fisherman birthday gags for his idea bank, but after he has a reserve on this theme, he probably won't buy another fisherman gag until he uses up his reserve. Your fisherman gag that you've kept circulating might get to him next year just at the time he decides it's time to buy another fisherman idea.

Another thing that will keep an editor from buying a fairly good idea is Ye Olde Budget. Most greeting card editors have only so much money that they can spend for freelance ideas, and when the money begins to run short they often pass up ideas that they wish they could have bought. Sometimes, if their budget is looser then, they'll grab the idea on its second time around. This type of thing very often happens with seasonal ideas.

Remember that each company has its own special requirements, likes, and dislikes. What won't sell to one company may often sell to another company.

Editors change frequently in the greeting card business, so it's possible that a company where your idea was once rejected might have a new editor who is just crazy about your kind of humor. Keep your ideas moving. They won't sell sitting in your file or in a box.

If you are submitting to a new editor or to one you've never submitted to before, and you don't know his requirements, likes, or dislikes, don't send him limited captions like birth, wedding, trip, or seasonal ideas. Send him some good everyday captions! These give you your greatest possibilities for sales, especially to new editors or with first-time submissions to a company.

There are, naturally, other things that you should perhaps do or not do, but you'll learn them as you go along.

Another thing you'll learn is that submitting ideas becomes quite a personal thing after a while. Some editors you'll become very friendly with, and you'll exchange ideas and news and generally chat through the mails.

Other editors, no matter how hard you try, will remain aloof and isolated. And even though you may sell ideas to them, you simply can't reach them on a friendly basis. They are never your enemies, but they're never your friends either.

All in all, submitting your material is an exciting part of the business. You'll reach the heights when your ideas are accepted, and you'll reach the depths when they are rejected. But, whichever way it is, it sure makes your mail a lot more exciting than getting letters from Aunt Agnes and Uncle Ralph.

Keeping
the Record
Straight

Although most writers dislike the mere thought of it, one of the most important parts of your freelance writing is keeping records of your material, where it is, where it has been, what has sold, what is available for submitting, what has been out too long, and a dozen other minor and major things. Along with the obvious importance of keeping records, it is also important that you don't spend too much time on this one part of your writing and thereby take time away from the actual creation of ideas. With this in mind, this chapter offers you quick and simple methods of keeping records. You may already have methods that suit you to a T, and if so, stay with them; but for those of you who do not, these are practical, usable methods that will work for you *now*. You may want to change or adapt them to your own personal likes and dislikes as you progress in your writing, and this is only normal since there is really no one best method of record keeping; but, in the meantime, try these.

Coding Your Ideas

Because your greeting card ideas do not have titles as stories do, you should assign a code number to each idea. This makes it easy for the editor to refer to your idea, both in his correspondence with you and on all those checks he'll be sending you.

There are three basic ways of coding an idea. The first is a simple *numerical code* in which you number your ideas in sequence, such as 1, 2, 3, 4, or 101, 102, 103, etc. Some writers prefix the number with one or more letters that stand for the type of idea it is; for example, B for Birthdays, GW for Get Wells, A for Anniversaries, and so on. A birthday number might be numbered B-501; a get well GW-356; and an anniversary, A-234.

The basic problem with this method is that it is necessary to keep track of the last number you used so that you can continue to number your ideas in sequence. Some writers don't like this coding system, because they feel that an editor can tell an old idea because of the low number it might have in relation to the other ideas in the batch.

The second method is to *number* the ideas by *batch* or *set*. In this method, the set of ideas is given an arbitrary number like B10. The first card in the set is then numbered B10-1, the second card B10-2, the third B10-3, and so on. If card number B10-2 is sold, then a new idea is put into its place and given the number B10-2. Thus the cards can be kept track of by *sets*.

The third method is an *alphabetical code*. The code is derived by using the first letter of the first three words in the main body of your idea (the main body being that part which immediately follows a standard opening like "For your birthday," or "Because it's your birthday"). These three letters are then coupled with the letters standing for the type of idea it is (B for birthday, etc). For example, if the idea started out "I know that your birthday . . .", we would take the first letter from each of the words, "I know that," put a B in front of it, and come up with B-IKT, and that would be the code number of the idea. An idea that started "No wonder you're sick" would be coded GW-NWY. This is probably the fastest and easiest coding method because it can be done while you're making up your dummy or card for submission, and it isn't necessary to keep track of the last code number you used because they have no bearing on one another.

Regardless of which method you use, don't number every idea you write since you will be writing many more ideas than you will actually be submitting. Only number your ideas when you have them ready for submission. And don't forget to put the same code number on your file copy of the idea.

Keeping Track of Where Your Ideas Have Been

For each idea you submit, make up a 3x5 file card. Put the code number of the idea on the front of the card along with the idea itself. On the back of the card, record where you're sending the idea. The simpler the method of recording, the better, because it saves valuable time. Always abbreviate the name of the company.

For example, P for Paramount, RC for Rust Craft, G for Gibson, and so on down your submission list.

The first item on the back of the file card should include the company, the month, and the year, like this: G3-81. This means the idea went first to Gibson in March of 1981. The next time it goes out, simply jot the company abbreviation down. If it is the next month or later, put down the new month in addition to the company abbreviation. Don't put down a new month or year until it changes. If some editor holds the idea or comments on it, note this next to the company when the idea comes back. When you sell the idea, record the actual date of sale, and the purchase price. A short record on the back of your card might look like this:

G3-81
RC—Held 4/5/81, Ret. 4/20/81
P4—Sold 4/28/81—$50

When the idea is sold, put the file card into a *sold* file under the company it was sold to. This makes it easy to refer to any idea bought by a particular company, and also makes a handy reference file of the kind of ideas that each company is buying from you.

Keeping Track of Ideas You Are Submitting

Put the file cards of ideas you are submitting to one company together; then take another card and type on it the name of the company, the number of ideas in the batch, and the date the batch was mailed. Since you may have thirty or forty batches in the mail, and several to the same company, put a *sequence* number on the card also. This sequence number will be the number of batches you have out. If this is the thirtieth batch you have in the mails, put the number 30 on the card. Secure the card with a rubber band to the batch of file cards and file the whole thing in sequence after the last batch under the general title of *Submitted*.

Now put the sequence number somewhere on the back of your return envelope. When your envelope comes back you will be able to match it quickly with the proper batch of file cards, which will keep you, perhaps, from having to paw through the whole mess to match up some of the returned ideas to file cards.

Sending Queries about Ideas That Have Been Out Too Long

If a batch has been out more than six weeks without any word from the editor, then send a polite query, enclosing a stamped self-addressed envelope (SASE), asking him to check on the status of your ideas. This will ordinarily bring a prompt reply. If you still do not hear within another two weeks, send another query, again enclosing the SASE, and mentioning that this is the second query. If you still do not get an answer (and, unfortunately, there occasionally is an editor who ignores, or is ignorant of, even the basic courtesies to writers), then send the editor a letter stating that if you don't hear from him within ten days, your ideas (list them) are no longer for sale at his company.

Some writers always register this type of letter and request a return receipt. In any case, for future reference, always keep a copy of your letter and of the ideas you submitted.

If you haven't received an answer from the editor by the end of two weeks (allow a few extra days for good measure), make up new roughs and start submitting them to other companies.

What to Do about Batches That Come Back with Ideas Missing

There are a few editors who at times hold ideas out of a batch without mentioning it. Or it sometimes happens that the editor simply forgets to do so. For that reason, *always* count the number of ideas in any returning batch *immediately,* before they have a chance to get mixed up with anything else.

If the editor who has held the ideas decides to buy them, he will either send you a check or a letter/invoice telling you he is buying your ideas. You simply sign the invoice that is at the bottom of the letter and return it to him. Soon after, you receive your check in the mail. (If you *don't* receive your check within thirty days after an editor tells you he is buying something, or after you have returned the invoice, send a polite query about it. Thirty days is long enough to wait.) If he is not going to buy your ideas, he will, of course, return them to you.

There might be times when an editor will write to you and say that he is buying your idea number so-and-so for so much money (he'll give a rate) and ask you to send him an invoice for the idea. If this happens, you can buy a pad of invoices (statements) at most department and stationery stores. All you do then is type out the editor's name and company at the top of the invoice, put down the code number of the idea and the idea itself, list the price the editor gave you, sign it, and send it in to him. He'll send you a check.

Now, besides the editor holding ideas from your batch, it is also possible, of course, that your ideas have been lost or misplaced. So if ideas are missing and you don't hear anything about them within four to six weeks, a polite query is certainly in order.

Under any condition, the best rule to follow with editors is: When you are in doubt about something, *ask!* Time permitting, you will usually get an answer of some kind. If an editor answers and says that he doesn't have your ideas, don't argue with him. He has no reason to lie to you. Keeping your ideas doesn't put money into his pocket. Just make up new roughs and start submitting them again.

If You've Run Out of Companies and Your Idea Hasn't Sold

If this happens to you—and if it doesn't, you're a better writer than most—*don't* throw the idea away. Put it away in your file; and then, about a year from the date you sent it to the first company on your list, start it circulating again. You may even find, before you start recirculating it, that you can now see how to improve it, because you will obviously have improved yourself during this time. Above all: *Never give up on any idea as long as you believe it is a good one!* Always keep your ideas going, revising and updating when you can . . . and remember, it may sell on its next time out!

Filing Seasonal Ideas and Ideas That Haven't Sold

The most simple and straightforward method of filing inactive material is to file the ideas under general categories of *birthday, get well, friendship, anniversary, Christmas, Valentine's Day, Easter,* and so on. Some writers break their files down further into specific captions like *wife birthday, masculine get well, better-half anniversary,* etc., but this can become very time consuming. Try the simpler method of filing ideas by general categories first, and see how it works for you. Then if you feel like you want to break the ideas down further into specific captions, it should be fairly easy to switch over.

What to Do if You Find a Published Card Identical to an Idea You've Just Sold

The best thing to do is to write the editor who bought your idea and tell him exactly what has happened. If you have not yet been paid for your idea, he will probably stop payment. If the check is on the way to you, return it when you receive it. If you've already received the check and cashed it, the simplest thing, from a bookkeeping standpoint, is for you to replace the idea with the next one the editor picks to buy. This is usually what is done. The editor discards, or returns, the original idea, and then gets a free one from you—his choice, of course. If some time has passed and your idea has been published before you spot the identical card, there is obviously nothing that can be done about it, and so there is no reason to call it to the editor's attention, but this is another good reason to study the markets constantly.

Remember, part of an editor's job is constantly to study cards on the market, and it sometimes happens that he spots a card that he has just purchased from a writer. This duplication can happen through pure accident, of course, and it frequently does; but if it happens too often to the same writer, the editor will become leery of that writer's work. Make certain that writer isn't you by reading and researching published cards as often as you can.

Releases

Some editors still write to writers and ask them for a release for certain of their ideas that the editor wants to buy. The *release* they are looking for is the same thing that appears on the back of most payment checks for ideas. It is simply a statement that your idea is original, that it has never been sold to anyone else, and that you release all rights to the idea upon payment of the check. To send the editor the release, simply type a statement to that effect, sign it, and send it to him. He'll send you a check.

Income, Expenses, and Taxes

After a company has purchased a number of ideas from you, it may either ask you for your Social Security number or assign a freelance writer's number to you. At the end of the year it will send you a tax form and also report having paid you X number of dollars to the infernal revenue service. When you start selling like crazy all those fabulous ideas of yours, it would probably behoove you, somewhere along the line, to have a tax expert advise you on what to report, what expenses to keep track of, what taxes you will have to pay, and, most important for you, all those nice things you can deduct. Point: *Don't wait until January to do it!*

How
to Tame
a Wild Editor

by Golly

E ditors are funny animals. Ask anyone who's ever tried to feed and care for one. They live on a strict diet of greeting card ideas—but not just *any* greeting card ideas. No, they're *choosy* critters. They'll only accept certain kinds of ideas. Each editor has his own personal taste, and it seems that you can never be sure, from day to day, just what he's going to take a liking to.

Usually editors are docile creatures. Sometimes they even seem a bit cold and indifferent. But they can get riled up from time to time, and when that happens, well, it's hard to get them to even *look* at your ideas. And if you're trying to make a living feeding an animal that won't eat, you've got *big problems.*

Editors are funny animals. They can seem *easy* to please and *impossible* to please. Of course the best way to keep them pleased is to give them a regular supply of the kinds of ideas they're most likely to love. And it doesn't hurt to *avoid* feeding them some of the things that give them indigestion. When editors get indigestion they're just no fun at all. So to help you to keep them happy, here are a few pointers, a few **do's** and **don't's** on the proper care and feeding of a wild editor:

Do *always send an SASE* (self-addressed stamped envelope). Whether you're submitting ideas or asking for information, an SASE makes an editor's job easier, and makes him tend to like you better. Some editors will simply not respond to a question that comes in without an SASE. It's understandable, considering that an editor's freelance correspondences run well into the thousands each year. Imagine the cost to his company if the editor had to hire someone to type return envelopes and put postage stamps on each one!

Don't *send letters to your editors telling them what a great writer you are or what great ideas you have.* Editors can't buy on the basis of your reviews. They buy verses individually on the merits of the idea itself. Even the old pros have to keep producing fresh, new ideas. It's not like the novel business where once you've made your name you can sell just about anything.

Do *keep informed of the editor's needs.* Ask for a current needs list from time to time. Ask questions of your editor if any come up. Just word the question in such a way that it's easy to understand, and capable of being answered in very few words. Don't ask questions like, "Why aren't you buying from me?" or "How can I write better verses?" It takes books like this to answer those types of questions. No editor has time to go into detail about a writer's attributes and faults. If he did it for one writer, it's only fair that he do it for all. And there aren't enough hours in a lifetime to do that!

Don't *tell editors you've decided to write greeting cards because there weren't any good ones out there. . . .* Even if you feel that way about it (and let's face it, we all come into this business thinking we can write better stuff than what's out there), it still pays to show a little tact. Many of those crummy cards you're criticizing were probably written by that editor. It's foot-in-mouth time!

Do *study the market regularly.* Keep abreast of what's out on the card racks. They give you a feel for what the editors are buying. They can also be a great source of ideas to rewrite or simply bounce off of.

Don't *scold an editor for not buying.* Nothing turns an editor off faster than that. Take this as a fact: Every editor *loves* to buy from freelancers. If they had their way they'd buy a lot from *every* writer and make *everybody* happy. It's only natural to want to make writers happy, because that, in turn, makes the writers like the editor, and we all want to be liked. But greeting card companies aren't philanthropic organizations to support struggling writers, and they don't have millions to throw around just for the sake of having popular editors. So, editors work with budgets, and budgets, being budgets, are always too small. The editor buys the best of what he can get with the money he's got. And if your ideas aren't the best he's getting, then don't turn your poison pen on him.

Do *keep your verses as widely sendable as possible.* No matter how clever your ideas may be, sendability is still an overriding factor in an editor's decision to buy. Many a funny studio gag has been turned down because of limitations in sendability. Keep this factor in mind: If you can leave out the word *I,* do so. You will have increased a card's sendability immensely. When you're doing special captions such as *Birthday, Mom,* make the idea sendable by children who may be either still at home or living elsewhere. If you mention what a great job Mom did of raising you, then you've just ruled out the possibility of that card's being sent by a married child. The child's spouse (who would normally be included in signing the card) was obviously not brought up by that Mom. Think about this kind of thing when you're writing. Increasing your card's sendability will increase its chances of selling to a sharp editor.

Don't *ask to be put on a mailing list.* Many companies don't have any such thing, and those who do reserve it for their experienced, reliable writers. If you establish yourself in this way, your editor won't have to be *told* to put you on his list. Don't confuse this with sending for current needs. Every writer should keep up on current needs. Just request that a needs list be included in with your returned ideas, or send an SASE.

Do *be sure to get the sending purpose identified on the outside of your cards.* With the exceptions of general birthday cards and general friendships, you should try to get the reason for sending the card right up front. Why? Because customers who are looking for a "Please Write" card often don't have the time to go through all of the cards looking for the one that says "Please Write" on the inside. If it's on the outside, the customer can find it right away. Editors will sometimes turn down very nice sentiments or very funny gags because the sending purpose can't be moved to the outside.

Don't *try to dictate the terms of sale to your editor.* Don't say that you have ten ideas that you will sell one-time rights to at $100 each, minimum purchase of three. The rules and terms of sale for greeting card ideas are well established, and there are enough good writers who accept these terms that an editor doesn't have to take revolutionaries seriously. If you want to play the game, follow the rules. The one exception to this is promotions, where, because of the complexities involved, each sale is negotiated on an individual basis.

Do *balance your submissions according to the editor's needs.* If you know from studying the market that an editor needs, say, ninety general birthday ideas for each "Please Write," then you should write about ninety birthday ideas for each "Please Write" that you create. The reason is this: You might send a batch of fifteen good "Please Write" cards. The editor might love three of them, but he's not likely to buy more than one. If they had been three birthday cards, he would no doubt have purchased all three!

Don't *turn ideas in a batch upside down or backwards to see if they're being read.* If anything, this very irritating practice will convince your editor *not* to read them.

Do *make sure that your idea is really a greeting card message, and not just a poem or a joke.* The me-to-you message is the soul of a greeting card. There have been, from time to time, cards that carried no me-to-you message, or perhaps an extremely subtle one. But these are too uncommon to be worth emulating.

Don't *warn editors against stealing your work.* They don't do that; they wouldn't have anything to gain by doing it; and they resent the suggestion that they might do it. But still, greenhorns (at least we hope that's what they are) insist on sending in warnings the likes of, "I will go to any length to protect my rights." A writer might just as well put in a note that says, "Don't buy any verses from me." Both notes have the same effect.

Do *try to be as fresh and original in your work as you can.* Some writers seem to have all the basics down, but their ideas are old and tired (just like most editors!). Fresh ideas are a must. They don't have to be crazy, off-the-wall things. Fresh new twists on old ideas are fine. Just so they're different—ideas the editor hasn't seen before.

Don't *accuse editors of stealing your gags.* This is worse than warning them not to do it. Every writer who has more than ten minutes of experience under his belt will write some ideas that have been covered by someone else before. Once again, editors do not steal ideas. They don't have any reason to. So if you see a verse that is similar to one that you had sent in, chalk it up to coincidence. The real fact of the matter may well be that the greeting card company owned that idea for twenty years before you sent yours in. It happens. It also happens that two or more writers send in virtually identical ideas on the same day. It's strange, and it leaves editors sitting around shaking their heads, but it happens.

Do *send in your ideas neatly typed or printed on clean, uniformly cut paper or cards.* Don't clutter up the front of your card with your name and address and such. It gets in the way of the sentiment. Put the record-keeping stuff on the back. And never send in any ideas that are old and faded, or covered with stuff from icky spills. No editor wants to touch it, much less buy it!

Don't *play on an editor's sympathies to get sales.* You've got your problems and the editor has his. He might sympathize with you but he can't spend the company's money to help you out of your woes.

Do *be patient with your editor.* Believe me, they've got to show a lot of patience themselves. Sometimes editors don't have time to let you know they're aware that you're out there. Most editors aren't really cold and methodical as those nasty old rejection slips might lead you to believe. It's just that no one's come up with a rejection slip yet that says, "Dear Writer, I'm a loving family person, and I'm really sorry that I can't buy your ideas, because I know what it's like when you've put so much into them . . ." There's really no need to go any further to see why rejection slips are kept rather formal. Editors really do care, believe it or not. But corporations aren't nearly so understanding, and they don't give the editors more than a few moments a day to read and respond to up to 500 freelance ideas. It's mind boggling at times—500 ideas in about 90 minutes. The best an editor can do is to be efficient, and hope the writer understands.

Don't *plagiarize.* It's unethical and illegal. End of sermon!

I can't promise that these suggestions will turn all of your ideas into best-selling gems, but following the rules sure can't hurt. And who knows? All of a sudden one day all those mean grouchy editors might start taking notice that you're feeding them just the kinds of ideas they've been asking for. And the next thing you know, they're being as sweet as can be. Editors *can* be tamed, you know—like most funny animals!

Glossary
of
Greeting Card Terms

Action: The items or process that produce a movement or effect.

Action card: A card that contains an action, such as a **pop-up** or slider.

Art director: The person who directs the functions of the art department; usually responsible for both staff and freelance artwork.

Artwork: The illustrations and lettering on a greeting card.

Attachment: An object fastened or attached to a greeting card.

Batch: A group of card ideas submitted together in one envelope.

Beading: A coating or finish consisting of small glass or plastic beads.

Black and white: The basic card illustration sketched by the artist without color. Looks somewhat like a black and white cartoon.

Body humor: Humor based upon functions or actions of or upon the body that are outside the realm of sex humor; e.g., belly button and bedpan gags would be body humor.

Buildup: The first part of a gag that sets the reader up for the punchline. Sometimes called **lead-in** or feed line; usually given entirely on the cover or outside of a card.

Caption: Ordinarily, the specific purpose or individual for which the card is intended: for example, Mother—Mother's Day, Female—Birthday, Girl—Graduation. The caption may at times designate the individual or group sending the card: for example, Mother's Day—From Daughter, Get Well—From Group.

Card code: A numerical or alphabetical indicator assigned to a specific verse or gag as a means of rapid identification.

Category: A broad grouping or classification used to designate cards for similar occasions: for example, Birthday, Anniversary, Get Well, and Friendship are all separate categories.

Color separation: (1) A photographic process in which colors are separated or isolated through the use of color filters; (2) a mechanical process in which the artist opaques (blacks) in on a sheet of acetate (a clear plastic material) the area where a color is desired. Opaquing is done for each color on the card. When sent to the engraver, the opaqued areas become solid raised areas on the printing plate. Ink of the desired color is then used to coat the raised areas. The ink is transferred to the paper by pressure, and the operation is repeated for each color. The printing process is similar to that employed when you use a rubber handstamp.

Contemporary: (1) **Studio**; (2) belonging to the present time.

Conventional: Formal or sentimental cards, done in rhymed verse or prose.

Cover: The front of a card, sometimes called the **outside** or page 1.

Creative director: Person in charge of the creative department.

Cutes: (1) Soft humored, slightly sweet feminine-type cards in which the text is closely tied to the illustration—physically, may be varying sizes; (2) **informals.**

Design: (1) The whole layout of a greeting card, including illustrations, type of lettering, color, and placement of all of these on the card; (2) **artwork.**

Die-cut: Cutting a card into some other than its normal shape—e.g., in the shape of an animal illustrated on the cover, or cutting holes in the card.

Dummy: A form shaped like a greeting card with a rough illustration and lettering, used to submit ideas.

Editor: Person in charge of editorial department and/or responsible for all the ideas in a particular line, such as studio line; may also write a portion of the line.

Editorial director: Head of editorial department that consists of several editors, writers, and clerks.

Engraver: The person who forms the artwork impressions upon the metal plates in preparation for printing.

Everydays: Cards for occasions that occur *every day* of the year, such as birthdays and anniversaries.

Finish: (1) A completed card design, including final artwork, color separation, and lettering; (2) material used on the cover of a card—e.g., flocking or beading.

Flocking: A material having a feltlike feel and appearance, used as a finish on a card.

French fold: A method of folding used for humorous and conventional cards. The basic fold consists of using a sheet of paper four times the final size of the card, folding the paper in half, *down,* and then folding the resultant sheet in half *across.* Also used for multipage cards. The purpose of this fold is to allow all printing to be done on one side of the paper only. French fold is a less expensive method when color is used on inside illustrations, as is often done on conventional and humorous cards.

Gag: See **idea.**

General: See **conventional.**

Holds: Denotes the ideas an editor retains for further consideration or for a product or line planning meeting.

Humor formula: A loosely set category for designating a type of joke or gag.

Humorous: A card in which the sentiment is expressed humorously. Text may be in either verse or prose, but is most often in verse. The illustration is usually tied closely to the text, and much of the humor is derived from the illustration itself. Published in various sizes; often illustrated with animals.

Idea: Used synonymously with **verse** or **gag,** especially for studio cards.

Idea bank: A reserve or surplus of ideas that an editor has bought but has not yet published.

Informals: See **cutes.**

Inside left: Counting the cover of a normal two-fold card as page 1, the *inside left* would be page 2, and the back of the card would be page 4.

Inside right: Page 3 of a normal two-fold card—see **inside left.**

Invoice: A statement listing the code number of your idea, the idea itself, and the price the editor has offered for it.

Juveniles: Cards designed to be sent to children, usually up to about age 12. Mostly written to be sent *from* adults.

Lead-in: See **buildup.**

Letterer: A person who marks or draws the letters and numbers on a card.

Line: (1) A row of words in a verse; (2) the words on the cover of a studio card, *or* the words on the inside—commonly called *outside line, inside line;* (3) all of the same types or series of cards published by a company, usually broken down roughly into broad grouping—e.g., studio line, humorous line, everyday line, Christmas line, etc. A very general classification.

Local imprints: Cards that are intended to be sent from a specific city or area. Cards are usually headed with something like: "Hello from. . . ." Name of city or area is left out when cards are initially printed. It's specifically imprinted when cards are ordered.

Market letter: The list of categories and themes an editor needs items for. Some companies publish market letters on a regular basis, others only when the need arises.

Mechanical: Pertains to a card that contains an action of some type.

Needs: Types of ideas an editor requires, or *needs.*

Neuter: A character depicting neither sex; could be either male or female.

Novelty: Refers to items that fall outside the realm of greeting cards (such as buttons, posters, plaques), although they may be sent for the same occasion as greeting cards, and they may be boxed differently and sold at different prices from standard greeting card prices.

Outside: The front of a card, also called the **cover.**

Pop-up: A mechanical action in which a form protrudes from the inside of the card when the card is opened.

Premise: The basic idea around which a verse or gag is built.

Promotions: Usually a series or group of cards (though not confined to cards) that have a common feature and are given special sales promotion.

Prose: The ordinary language used in speaking and writing, as opposed to verse and poetry.

Punchline: That last part of a gag or joke in which the denouement is contained.

Punch-out: Section of a card—usually a juvenile, but also sometimes a studio or humorous card—that is perforated so it can be easily removed.

Rates: The amount that an editor pays for each line of verse or for an overall idea.

Reader: The person reading the card.

Receiver: The person who receives the card.

Recipient: See **receiver.**

Rejects: The ideas or verses that have not been purchased by the editor and are returned.

Rejection slip: Two dirty words.

Requirements: See **needs.**

Return envelope: A self-addressed stamped envelope **(SASE)** that you include with the batch or request you submit so that the editor can return rejected ideas or requested material to you.

Risqué: Ideas that joke suggestively about sex.

SASE: Self-addressed stamped envelope.

Seasonals: Cards published for the several special days that we observe during the year—e.g., Christmas, Graduation, Halloween.

Sendability: Pertains to the degree to which a particular idea or card is appropriate for a specific occasion and for the largest possible number of senders and receivers.

Sender: The person who sends the card.

Series: A limited number of cards in which there is something—such as theme, action, attachment, or finish—held in common by all.

Sex humor: Humor based upon male/female sex relations.

Slam: Insulting humor.

Spinner: A device that spins, sometimes pointed at the end or in the shape of an arrow.

Staff writer: A writer who works full time for a company, on company premises, and is paid a salary.

Statement: See **invoice.**

Studio: (1) **Contemporary;** (2) cards that use short, punchy gags that are in keeping with current humor trends. Always rectangular in shape.

Suggestive humor: Sex humor, body humor, or mild profanity contained in a card.

Tag line: The line or words that designate the occasion and transmit the wish or basic sentiment: for example, Happy Birthday, Get Well Soon, Merry Christmas, Happy New Year. The tag line is usually either the first or the last line on the card.

Theme: The subject or topic of a verse or gag: for example, love, drinking, sex, compliment.

Three-fold: A card that is folded twice, just as you would fold a business letter. The last fold, or section, may be folded either inward to the center of the card or outward to the back of the card.

Timely: Ideas or cards containing subjects that are seasonably or opportunely timed. Sometimes used to mean **topical,** but should not be; ideas using Tiny Tim as a subject would be *timely* for Christmas, *untimely* for Halloween, and *topical* for neither.

Toilet humor: See body humor.

Topical: Ideas or cards containing subjects that are currently the topic of discussion. Sometimes used in the same sense as **timely,** but should not be. A subject may be timely because of the season (e.g., witches at Halloween) but not be of sufficient interest to be a general topic of discussion.

Vari-vue: Trade name for flat, glasslike devices that appear to contain moving illustrations—for example, female lips that are either pursed or smiling, depending on the angle at which you view the device. Also can contain such illustrations as bucking horses, flying witches, vibrating hearts, and winking eyes.

Verse: Usually refers to a line of poetry that has a metrical or rhythmical pattern, but at times used to mean any text on a card. Thus a studio card gag written in prose might be referred to as a verse.

Virko: A shellac-type finish on cards.

Wish: (1) To express a desire that someone have happiness, good fortune, good will, or good health; (2) to express a desire or yearning for someone or something.

Bibliography

Evans, Bergen, and Evans, Cornelia. *A Dictionary of Contemporary American Usage.* Random House, 201 East 50th St., New York NY 10022.

This is one of the most useful dictionaries there is on word preference, style, grammar, punctuation, and just plain common sense in the use of words. It's a great book, easy to read and easy to understand.

Morris, William, and Morris, Mary. *Harper Dictionary of Contemporary Usage.* Harper and Row, Publishers, Inc., 10 East 53rd St., New York NY 10022.

Here is another outstanding dictionary on contemporary usage.

Bartlett's Familiar Quotations. Little, Brown and Company, 34 Beacon St., Boston MA 02106.

This is probably the best of several collections of old and new quotations. There must be thousands of ideas for conventional verses in this book, as well as hundreds of ideas that could be switched into studio cards. Any one of the ideas could pay you more than what the book costs.

The Holy Bible.

The world's greatest source of material for inspirational verses, and also for conventional verses. Using only this book, you should never run out of ideas for either type of verse. A word of advice: When quoting from the Bible be sure to mention which version you are using, and give book, chapter, and verse.

Wentworth, Harold, and Flexner, Stuart Berg. *Dictionary of American Slang.* Thomas Y. Crowell Company, 10 East 53rd St., New York NY 10022.

This book contains a treasury of slang words and expressions that people are now using. It is an invaluable book to the studio card writer, who is often dependent upon the meaning and usage of a particular slang word. The money this book costs could easily come back to you in the first sale of a gag containing a slang term or word that you used in the right way. It's available through the Writer's Digest Book Club.

Roget's International Thesaurus. Thomas Y. Crowell Company, 10 East 53rd St., New York NY 10022.

If you use words and you don't want to use the same ones over and over, you need this book. It's as simple as that.

Sutphen, Dick. *Old Engravings and Illustrations.* The Dick Sutphen Studio, Inc., Box 628, Scottsdale AZ 85252.

This book is only one of a series of books that contain copyright-free (meaning anyone can use them for any purpose, free of charge) engravings and illustrations. The books are great for illustrating humorous and studio gags. Most of the books in the series cost $10.00 plus, but some are less. Mr. Sutphen has a brochure describing the books. Send for it.

The Writer. The Writer, Inc., 8 Arlington St., Boston MA 02116.

A writer who doesn't subscribe to a writer's magazine has got to be a little weird. Don't be! *The Writer* runs a lot of good articles on greeting cards and light verse. Also contains up-to-date market lists and a good market letter.

Writer's Digest. F&W Publishing Corporation, 9933 Alliance Rd., Cincinnati OH 45242.

This book that you are now reading, from which you've learned all those great things that will make you a fortune, is published by Writer's Digest Books. If you don't subscribe to *Writer's Digest* magazine, don't talk to us! In fact, don't even read this book—you don't deserve it.

Greetings Magazine. 95 Madison Ave., New York NY 10016.

An appropriate name for the greeting card industry's own trade magazine.

Webster's New Collegiate Dictionary. G. & C. Merriam Company, Springfield MA 01101.

The standard, most professional desk dictionary.

Webster's New World Dictionary of the American Language. (Second College Edition). The World Publishing Company, 119 West 57th St., New York NY 10019.

Especially helpful, as it gives all the different ways a word can be spelled, including the plural, the *-ing* and *-ed* endings, and all the rest. Available from the Writer's Digest Book Club.

Also buy collections of verses put out by many greeting card companies. And try the collections of some of our popular poets, like Robert Frost and Carl Sandburg.

The National Association of Greeting Card Publishers (600 Pennsylvania Ave., S.E., Washington, D.C. 20003) is a group of nice, helpful people who offer a lot of good things to help writers. Write to them and ask.

You might also do well haunting used bookstores, looking for collections of epigrams, jokes, anecdotes, quotations, humorous stories, verses, and anything else that might supply inspiration for your work. Used books are generally not too expensive, so you can build up a good collection that way. In addition, there is always the possibility of your finding an out-of-print collection that no other greeting card writer has. It could turn out to be your own personal gold mine.

Contributors

Florence Bradley: While taking a correspondence course in fiction writing, Florence Bradley was advised by her instructor to subscribe to *Writer's Digest*. She did. In it she found a market list of greeting card companies, and she started writing greeting cards. Although not an instant success, Florence kept at it. As a result, she has sold several hundred greeting cards, almost half of them juvenile cards. Raising six children has helped give her ideas and a ready-made testing panel for her juvenile cards. Florence has branched out from greeting cards in recent years. She has been a reporter and photographer for the *Atlantic City Press* for 5½ years. She has written award-winning juvenile and nonfiction articles and has recently completed a children's book, *A Valentine Surprise*. Her latest accomplishment is the completion of her first adult novel, *Go for the Juggler,* which she hopes to have published soon. She is currently living in Ocala, Florida, where she has opened a gift shop.

Patricia Ann Emme: A freelance writer of verses and inspirational material for greeting cards, magazines, and booklets for the past twelve years, Patricia Ann Emme is one of those rare people who puts her heart and soul into her work. She says that writers "have a responsibility to bring beauty and faith to others through their written work, and not to discredit others or take away the joy found in words." One need only read one of her inspirational verses to see that she finds joy and gives a lot of it to others through words. Her conventional and inspirational verses appear on cards for Paramount, Warner Press, Rust Craft, American Greetings, Freedom Greetings, Norcross, Hallmark, Gibson, Buzza, Mark I, Gallant, and Sangamon. In addition, she has won several prizes for her poetry, and is listed in *Who's Who in Poetry*. As would be expected of one who appreciates the beauty in words, she's also an avid reader.

Bernice Gourse: Bernice Gourse is the Director of Editorial for the Paramount Line, Inc., in Pawtucket, Rhode Island. She is one of the most knowledgeable people in the business today, and for good reason—as the daughter of Samuel Markoff, founder of the Paramount Line, she has literally grown up with the business. Bernice graduated from Pembroke College in Brown University in 1941 and worked for Paramount as an editorial clerk until her marriage in 1946. After twenty years, during which time she raised two children and was active in numerous community service activities, she returned to Paramount as co-editor with her sister, Dorothy Nelson. She became director of editorial in 1977. Bernice says that she thoroughly enjoys her work in the editorial end of greeting cards—particularly the daily contact with the wide horizons of human emotions. But she laments not having enough hours in a day to pursue other forms of writing and art. She does, whenever possible, share two favorite hobbies with her husband—travel and nature photography.

Bob Hammerquist: Native of Brockton, Massachusetts. Freelance gag writer and cartoonist, and successful neighborhood ne'er-do-well. Connoisseur of domestic beers, and semi-professional Scotch quaffer. Journeyman cynic. Docile militant. Three-martini-liberal. Upholder of the Donald Duck ethic. Devastating critic of the immaterial. Honorary Chairman of the Bulgarian Friends of the D.A.R. Currently researching his next literary illusion, an already lightly dismissed probe of the American religious conscience, entitled: "Church Franchises for Profit and Prophet *or* How to Have Your Wafer and Eat It Too." (Editor's note: Bob wrote the above for himself, but he forgot to mention that he is also one of the top studio card writers in the country . . . and he's not bad in the city, either.)

Laurie Kohl: Editing for Gibson Greeting Cards since 1970, Laurie Kohl has had experience in every type of greeting card writing, from studio to inspirational. Most of her editing experience has been in the conventional cards, where she now makes her home editing and writing for Gibson's everyday line. Laurie first came into the world of greeting cards in 1951, when, as a co-op student in advertising design at the University of Cincinnati, she made color separation drawings for Gibson. After marrying and living in various parts of the country as an Air Force and airline wife, she returned to Cincinnati. She did some freelance writing during her years of moving around, and in 1968, back in Cincinnati, she went to work for Gibson as a writer. She's been involved in the writing and editing ends of greeting cards ever since. In her leisure time (what little there is of that for us overworked editors), Laurie has taken up running (she calls it jogging). She also told me that she's the grandmother of the cutest baby in the world, knowing, of course, that it wouldn't be printed, since I have two little ones of my own.

Dick Lorenz: As Editorial and Humor Manager for Norcross Greeting Cards before it went out of business, Dick Lorenz had overseen and managed all Norcross editorial functions and had art-directed all humor and studio cards. Dick was with Norcross for more than twenty-two years, during which time he had worked as a writer and artist, writing copy for all types of greeting cards. He had done most of his work in humorous, studio, and informal cards. Prior to his work at Norcross, Dick attended Syracuse University, where he earned a bachelor's degree in Fine Arts.

Richard E. Myles: Director of Creative Planning and Editorial for more than three years at Rust Craft Greeting Cards in Dedham, Massachusetts, before it went out of business, Richard E. Myles had been responsible for the activities of the editorial and creative planning departments. In his seventeen previous years with Rust Craft, he had worked in Product Planning, Stock Control, and advertising. Before joining Rust Craft, Dick had worked for eight years as an editor and reporter for the *Providence Journal-Bulletin,* Providence, Rhode Island. During a two-year stint in the U.S. Navy, he had worked for Armed Forces Radio and Television. Dick holds a bachelor of arts degree from the University of Notre Dame. As a hobby he has collected a personal library of more than 5,000 books.

Larry Sandman: Though a mere youngster of less than thirty (and holding), Larry Sandman has had experience in all types of greeting card writing. Now editor of the studio and humorous lines for Gibson Greeting Cards, Larry started in 1976 as a writer. A 1975 graduate of Miami University, Larry was one of the few people who already knew they wanted to become greeting card writers before coming out of school. Larry lives on a mini-farm in Bright, Indiana, where he grows corn, tomatoes, pumpkins, melons, and two sons. Among his interests are sports, juvenile literature (it's at his reading level), and country living. His favorite activity is going home from work and sitting around looking tired.

Index